Teaching Day by Day

180 STORIES TO HELP YOU
ALONG THE WAY

DONALD H. GRAVES

Foreword by Nancie Atwell

HEINEMANN

Portsmouth, NH

To

Nancie Atwell *and* Mary Ellen Giacobbe

good colleagues and friends for twenty-five years

Heinemann
A division of Reed Elsevier, Inc.
361 Hanover Street
Portsmouth, NH 03801–3912
www.heinemann. com

Offices and agents throughout the world

Cataloging in publication data on file at the Library of Congress.

ISBN: 0-325-00598-2

Editor: Lois Bridges
Cover photography and design: Catherine Hawkes, Cat & Mouse Design
Author photo: Kucine Photography
Manufacturing: Steve Bernier

Printed in the United States of America on acid-free paper
07 06 05 04   VP   1 2 3 4 5

CONTENTS

PART ONE

In the Beginning

PART TWO

The Teacher Makes the Difference

PART THREE

Family Matters

PART FOUR

Learning from Children

PART FIVE

Supporting Reading and Writing

PART SIX

Getting Personal

PART SEVEN

Thinking About Learning

PART EIGHT

Thinking About Assessment

PART NINE

Full Circle

FOREWORD

I love this man. I love these stories.

Teachers know Donald Graves the researcher as a master storyteller. His studies of children's writing transformed our profession because Don journeyed to schools, lived in classrooms, and reported his findings as stories that revealed young writers and their teachers at work. Readers recognized the students, identified with the teachers, and, fueled by the power of Don's stories and the theories he inferred, changed the way we teach writing. His many friends who know Graves beyond the page recognize that he and the methodologies of descriptive research are a match made in heaven. He is a born collector of stories.

Now, the tables are turned. Teachers get to live inside Don's classroom—or, rather, an abundance of his classrooms, literal and figurative. Stories are the medium for the lessons; narrative is how he seeks—and finds—meaning in his life.

In these 180 essays, Graves plumbs a remarkable range of meanings through stories that are literary, political, scholarly, and humorous but always personal. Again and again he reminds me of the single most surprising thing that good stories can do: through the rich specifics of his experience, Don calls up my own memories of teaching, childhood, college, family, and marriage. He compels me to consider how my accumulated experiences have made me who I am today and to embrace my own stories, good and bad.

Don's honesty as a storyteller is bracing. The tales he tells on himself show how painful learning from life can be. They also reveal a person so alive, so intoxicated with all the world has to offer, so interested and so interesting, that he challenges us, by his example, to want to be like him. And that is one of the marks of a great teacher.

In this book, Graves introduces us to his great teachers. We see how he learned to read our culture from the work and words of such artists as musician Winton Marsalis, painter Georgia O'Keefe, playwright Neil Simon, and poet Wislawa Zymborska. He shows us the life of his mind by gleaning gems of insight from physicists Nils Bors and Werner Heisenberg, systems theorist

Margaret Wheatley, historian David McCullough, and, especially, biologist Lewis Thomas. And he gives us snapshots of great classroom teachers at work, from Mary Ellen Giacobbe, Shelley Harwayne, Donald Murray, and Linda Rief to Miss Fitch, Ms. A., and the incomparable Donald Durrell.

Many of Don's stories end with pearls of advice for new teachers and old pros, applicable to the classroom as well as the teachers' lounge. Other stories capture the quiet moments of the life of a teacher—the emotional connections with children that drew the best of us to the profession in the first place. And some—my favorites—show Don before he was *Donald Graves:* his boyhood, early married life, first years of teaching, and quest to carve out an identity and be known for who he is. All the stories remind teachers to *pay attention,* to see the child, to understand the process, to acknowledge the context.

I know how I'll read *Teaching Day by Day.* I'll keep my copy on my bedside table so I can dip into it daily, just before sleep or after waking. I'm already craving the contemplative moments the stories will afford me amidst the busyness of my school year. At night, when I'm exhausted from a teaching day, it will be a comfort to have Don's words as my last thoughts. In the morning, a shot of Graves will give me energy for the teaching day ahead. The wisdom, humor, and compassion in these essays will give me resolve to be my best self in my classroom and school by reminding me, day by day, of what a privilege it is to spend a lifetime thinking about and being with children.

—Nancie Atwell

TO THE READER

For every book, there is a story about its beginning. Someone asked me, "Tell me about your first day of teaching."

"You don't want to hear it," I replied. "By ten a.m. I'd lost my lesson plan." That incident lingered and took me back to what got me into the teaching profession in the first place. I was just out of the service, I had one child, and another was on the way. I had to support them. I'd even taken a test through a psychological corporation that said that teaching was definitely something I ought not to do. But I was desperate, and teaching at least was in my family tradition. Fortunately, there was a teaching shortage at the time.

Telling these stories, I realized I was dealing with personal issues—the immediacy of the children I was teaching and my own growing family—as well as with the big picture of education. Telling stories and writing essays about issues has made my career as a teacher and educator much clearer. We need to acknowledge our stories and confront what we don't understand. Without our stories and the stories of colleagues, family, and friends, we lose out on both the big and small picture of daily living. Stories express what is human about us. Stories reveal fulfilled and unfulfilled wants. Our classrooms are points of intersection where many stories are worked out simultaneously.

Most everyone in the world around us, whether an administrator, a politician, or a used-car salesman, wants us to live her or his own unfolding story, whatever that may be. Unless we can say a loud yes to our own story and the direction in which our lives are headed we cannot provide effective responses to those around us. Of course, stories carry wonder, surprise, and humor in the remarkable discrepancies they reveal. Teaching is such an important responsibility that we have to learn to laugh.

It struck me that maybe I could write more stories and that they would trigger you to remember your own. A number crept in. Most school calendars are at least 180 days long. Why not write 180 essay/stories? I didn't know 180 stories, but maybe I could write 30 and see. Within a month I had 30 stories. And the more stories and essays I wrote, the more I found.

This book follows a loose timeline—there are very few temporal markers that show you what teaching day it is in the school calendar. Rather, the opening of the book is about my beginnings, both as a teacher and as an elementary school principal. The essays then proceed through personalities, zero in on the solid teaching of reading and writing, make a swing through assessment, and end up with a kind of a review.

You may sample these essays by yourself, in a leisurely fashion, pondering them and your own stories day by day. "I remember the time I . . ." is the ultimate gift you can give yourself. Or you may choose a colleague or a small group and read the book together. Read a story and say, "Has this happened to you? What's your version? How did you handle it? Can we think of a better way?"

However you go about it, I wish you a stimulating journey.

—Don Graves

ACKNOWLEDGMENTS

There are many people to acknowledge with regard to this book. Some are completely unaware of their contribution, others have been with me from the outset, from concept to fruition.

High on my list of "unawares" is Helen Porter, my first principal, who saw more in me than I saw in myself. She literally laughed me through my first year of teaching and then remained my supervisor when I replaced her as principal.

I also thank Donald Durrell, Boston University professor, who taught me the meaning of expectation, both of myself and of my students. Durrell was a no-nonsense, driving perfectionist, who expected nothing but the best from those around him. At some point in our careers we need to run into people like Durrell.

At a critical point in my career I landed by chance in the same building as Donald Murray on the University of New Hampshire campus, when the Early Childhood Program was housed not in the education building but in the English building. A friendship grew as Murray led me out of the arcane language of a dissertation into the real world of communication with texts that readers want to read. We have shared ideas, human predicaments, writing, and various books for the last thirty years.

I am most grateful to Rev. Dr. Gary Demarest, who taught me how to speak to real audiences. My learning was more an apprenticeship than the result of direct instruction. I saw how quickly he could reach a group and engage them in genuine, personal communication. He read audiences and congregations magnificently.

Anna Sumida was encouraging from the start, both of the idea and in her continual reading of the manuscript. It was Anna's suggestion that a concluding statement might bring home the point of each essay/story. I am grateful for this idea and her help.

Penny Kittle has critiqued the entire manuscript from start to finish. She is apt in sensing what I am trying to say and where I am trying to register my voice. She kept me on track by responding as a fan and being genuinely delighted by my stories. On the other hand she was forthright in putting her finger on contradictions as well as necessary repairs.

Camille Allen, Ardith Cole, and Jane Hansen read the entire manuscript and gave helpful, precise comments. Reading a colleague's manuscript very nearly exceeds the bounds of friendship. I am truly grateful for these friends and colleagues.

Nancie Atwell read beyond the manuscript, interpreting the text for what professionals need from day to day. She showed me where the book was both on and off target. She grasped this book's concept so well that I asked her to write the foreword. I am indebted to her for the gift of personal and professional friendship.

Cindy Marten has read selected pieces and given cogent responses while cheering me on to the end.

Maura Sullivan has read selected pieces and commented briskly on marketing strategies and ways teachers might use the book.

I am so pleased to have gotten to know Kären Clausen, who graciously handled the details of seeing this book through to production. She persisted in solving problems (many of which I'm probably not even aware) with charm and skill.

Lois Bridges is so bright a beacon in the lives of her writers that we hardly know how to thank her. She is my inspiration to keep writing. She has a genius for sensing the books her authors need to write. Lois has given me a whole new career in retirement thanks to her inspiring perceptions and constant good cheer. Getting out of bed to write in the morning is easy with an editor like Lois. I am so grateful to her for believing in me as a writer.

My dear wife Betty is my first reader. She is willing to drop what she is doing without hesitation, read the next piece, and give cogent comments. How fortunate I am to have had, for forty-nine years, a life companion who is a no-nonsense reader.

PART ONE

In the Beginning

We all remember our early days
of teaching. Whether they were but one or two years back or decades
ago, we never forget those formative (and often humorous, at least
in retrospect) incidents and the things they taught us. They are the
building blocks of our career. (I have also included stories from my
early days as a principal. Teachers need to be aware how much
young principals need their help!)

Above all, in this profession we've chosen, we need one another.
This is especially true of beginning teachers. I had the best of help
when I began teaching, but I still felt isolated. Much of that isolation
was my own doing. I needed to take the initiative in being a colleague,
but I didn't know how. There are specific things we can do to help
one another, whether we are just starting out or are already veterans.

Why a Teacher?

I was a snotty college English major. When my dad, a superintendent of schools, raised the question of my becoming a teacher, I couldn't say "Not on your life!" fast enough. I thought teaching was anti-intellectual and beneath my dignity. However, four years in the service, marriage, one child in hand and another on the way, sobered me. Suddenly teaching seemed the natural thing to do. It wasn't a complicated decision in which I pondered a host of other careers. I had to have a job and support my family.

And so I became the product of an eight-week summer intensive teacher preparation course. There was such an acute teaching shortage in 1956 that the state sponsored courses to fill the gaps in classrooms. They gradually prepared us for large classrooms by first having us work with small groups of children, then larger ones of as many as ten or fifteen. I enjoyed the children, and I liked teaching them new things and observing them learn.

One day that summer I was leaving the class to go out to the playground when quite suddenly and very naturally I felt a hand take mine. I looked down and saw a ten-year-old girl smiling up at me. It was such a simple connection, but I remember thinking, "Teaching is something wonderful." I'd met a side of myself I didn't know was there.

Teaching lets us develop a side of ourselves
we might never know otherwise.

The First Day

On my very first day of teaching I'd lost my lesson plan by ten a.m. I had worked for two days writing out that plan in order to be ready for my thirty-nine seventh graders. The principal who hired me had observed me teaching about a dozen ten-year-olds the summer before. She liked my teaching but the full meaning of her remark, "You won't be teaching a dozen children like that for a long, long time," didn't sink in until that first morning.

The children lay before me in waves, a sea of faces studying their new teacher. When I looked at them I didn't see individuals, just a mass of noisy adolescents. They all knew each other, having grown up together in our small semirural farming-fishing village. I followed my lesson plan for the first hour until it suddenly disappeared, stuck somewhere in a book or under the mass (mess?) of papers they'd already handed in. I never did find it. Maybe one of the children stole it.

But I had to get from ten o'clock to three o'clock, when the first busses began to pull out. So I told them stories of being in the U. S. Coast Guard the previous four years. I read aloud and asked them questions about what I'd read. I wanted to know what they thought. Gradually, my panic receded and individual faces emerged.

Our first day of teaching is invariably a blur of confusion, noise, and plans that don't work out as we'd envisioned.

The Detective Club

About six weeks into my first year of teaching the principal informed me that Mrs. Kennedy, the reading supervisor, would be in the next Monday to see me teach reading to my seventh graders. I didn't have much background in teaching reading, and I think I'd implied that I could probably use a little help.

I spent the entire weekend gearing up for my new creation, "The Detective Club." I set up a series of clues my students were to use to identify certain words, characters, incidents, and themes in the text they were reading. The children formed teams and, with great enthusiasm, shot into high-speed action. I knew how to pique children's interest, and all of them were marvelously engaged.

After class I met with Mrs. Kennedy and the school principal. Beaming, they told me how well they thought the lesson had gone. Just before our meeting ended Mrs. Kennedy asked, "And how are you going to follow up on this lesson tomorrow?" I'm usually quick with words, but the truth was I had given no thought at all to the next day's lesson. I mumbled something about continuing the Detective Club, but I had no idea how to do that.

Too often our lessons have absolutely no connection to the work of the day before or the day that follows. Let connectedness be one of our goals.

A Bumpy Flight

About five years ago I took a short flight in an eighteen-seat, propeller-driven aircraft from Albany, New York, to Boston, Massachusetts. The flight should have lasted thirty comfortable minutes. Instead, we flew through and around three thunderstorms. The plane felt out of control as we went up, down, and sideways, my stomach lurching as if I were in an elevator, my body straining against the seatbelt. The engines alternately raced and idled as the pilot tried to keep the plane headed toward Boston. Several women were crying, one of whom spoke no English. The flight attendant tried to soothe her, but the poor woman couldn't understand what was happening. When we finally landed, my body was quite literally shaking from head to toe. For a long time the slightest suggestion of airplane turbulence triggered warning signals first in my body, then in my thinking. People who have had automobile accidents report the same sensations. The body says, "Danger ahead."

In my early days of teaching, a challenge from a student would put my body and mind on similar alert. I didn't know what to do or say; I simply rode out the storm. Memories of these incidents stayed with me for days, weeks, even months. I was too ignorant then to know when or why a student felt cornered. Gradually, after years of these encounters, I began to be able to read the signs and head these disruptions off before they got out of hand.

Teachers need to anticipate when to shift to less
challenging approaches. Experience helps.

We Are Never Just Teachers

Our second daughter, Alyce, was born the second day of my first year of teaching. How delighted we were with little Alyce, who took in the world with her big eyes, and with Marion, our firstborn, who was saying her first words and pondering her new sister with a combination of delight and misgiving. Fortunately, Alyce didn't have colic as Marion had. But she still needed to be fed around the clock, and Marion was being toilet-trained.

We lived in a second-floor four-room apartment. I had a small table in the corner of our bedroom where I pounded out my lessons on a small, upright, noisy Royal typewriter. But I had to steal time for this only when the children were awake, because the sleep-disrupting typewriter easily penetrated the thin walls between the rooms.

I wasn't consciously aware of the emotional demands at the time, but I remember my emotional uptightness. I wondered if I'd survive my thirty-nine young adolescents. I had to be "up" for them, love little Alyce and Marion, and help my dear wife, who may have been saddled with a greater emotional load than I faced in the classroom. I'd sit at the kitchen table staring at a breakfast I often couldn't eat, thinking only of problem students and lesson plans, feeling quite sorry for myself. My father was my role model: he'd done the same thing at breakfast, staring off into space as he planned his moves on the job. I wish now I hadn't followed my father's lead, but my worry about the day ahead in the classroom stifled the present tense of attending to my family.

We are never just teachers. Our family, spouses, friends, and other loved ones are a center of our emotional energy as well.

Selling Encyclopedias

I was desperate to make some extra money after my first year of teaching (it wasn't easy supporting a wife and two children on an annual salary of $3100); the World Book encyclopedia company promised good money. Their strategy was simple; sell to the families of the children in your school. Doors opened quickly, because I was a respected teacher. I did very well for the first two weeks.

My pitch to parents was that the encyclopedias would help their children get the look-it-up habit, explore new knowledge, and do better in school. World Book is a good encyclopedia, but it wasn't long before I realized that some families were buying the books because of who I was, not because they knew how or intended to use them. They thought just having them on the shelf would magically turn their children into champion students. By the third week my conscience sapped my ability to sell. The district manager for World Book wondered what had gone wrong.

I decided just to visit homes instead (taking the selling prospectus with me in the unlikely case the subject of an encyclopedia came up). When I called to make an appointment, the reaction was often, "What's wrong? Is there something wrong with my child?" I immediately said, "I'm just calling to get to know you and your family."

And so I learned about the families in my school district. We chatted about their children, their likes and dislikes, their special skills and abilities I might never have encountered in the classroom. I uncovered the ethnic backgrounds—Portuguese, Finnish, Norwegian—of families busy in the fishing industry. I heard about bad-luck fishing trips that netted hardly enough money to tide the family over. I became acquainted with the new Australian method of milking cows in a milking parlor. I discovered the kinds of questions that would serve me well in my teaching career.

How fortunate we are when we can arrange to
learn about our children's lives firsthand.

The Note from Home

My colleague gave me a sidelong glance and said wryly, "I see you have Lucy W. next year in sixth grade. Lucy's okay, but her mother's a real problem." Sure enough, the second week of school Lucy passed me a note in near perfect handwriting. Her mother requested an appointment with me as soon as possible.

Mrs. W. did most of the talking, suggesting that Lucy had gone unappreciated throughout her school years and now she had a male teacher—me—who was somewhat intimidating. After listening for nearly twenty minutes, I managed to interject. "Tell me about Lucy at home."

"She reads quite a bit, and she does some rather remarkable needlepoint. Why do you ask? What's that got to do with school?"

"It has everything to do with school. I'm sure you're right, Mrs. W., we never do fully appreciate our children. Tell me how she learned to do needlepoint."

"It's always been in our family. I learned it from my grandmother, and Lucy learned it from me."

"I think it is wonderful that you do this together. Would you both consider coming to class and showing us your work?" Mrs. W. did come to school, and her work and Lucy's was remarkable. I hadn't realized that someone as young as Lucy could do such detailed and beautiful patterns. Lucy, her mother, and I had a good year after that.

Unless we ask, we won't know the many gifts children
have and the stories that lie behind them.

Our Foibles

I once watched a skit put on by our seventh graders. The boy playing me charged onto the stage, which was equipped with a desk—piled high with books and papers—and a chair. He was carrying a briefcase, which he plunked down next to the desk. Then he started to rummage through the papers. "It must be here somewhere," he bellowed to an imaginary class. The audience laughed, and so did I—it was a near-perfect imitation. He had my physical motions and language down pat.

I guess it shouldn't have been such a shock to me. Every day we are on display, and our students have to be able to interpret our moods and gestures for their own survival. Indeed, they laugh with one another about our foibles.

Penny Kittle (2003) says it best: "We are their entertainment."

An English Major Teaches Writing

There I was, that first year, an English major trying to teach seventh graders to write. As in most English departments the *summum bonum* of my college curriculum had been literature; the teaching of writing was left to graduate assistants and faculty wives. I went into teaching with a manner suggesting I was bringing enlightenment and salvation to the heathen.

I taught reading/literature four days a week and assigned writing on Fridays just after lunch. There was but one period between our rather late lunch break and the first busses. The students filed in, silently dreading the topic, which I'd written on the board and cleverly hidden behind the DeNoyer-Geppert map of the Soviet Union. I enjoyed the power their quietness gave me. I had the children trapped. Theoretically, they couldn't go home for the weekend unless they put a piece of writing in my hand as they left the room to get on the bus.

Fresh out of the military, I commanded, "Paper out, pencils at the ready." This meant all pencils were pointed toward the ceiling, points already sharpened. I then strode to the board and lifted the map so they could see the topic I'd chosen for the day: "Should There Be Capital Punishment?" When one of the students asked, "Mr. Graves, does that mean we capitalize everything?" I missed the real point of his question: he didn't have the foggiest notion what to write in response to the "morally uplifting" choice I'd made for him.

The children worked hard but didn't learn much. I corrected extensively but taught little. I took their papers home, corrected them, passed them back on Monday. They incorporated my corrections in a revised version on fresh white paper. It didn't dawn on me until the following March that I was correcting the same errors I had corrected in September.

Anyone can correct, but few can teach so the students
are able to revise and edit on their own.

The Book Is About Us

First-year teachers or those new to a school are the subject of a student-composed dossier by the first recess: "What's he like?" "Is she strict?" "Is he loud?" "What's she wearing?"

Nancie Atwell tells this story about herself. Every September she asks her students to estimate the number of books they read during the previous school year. One June, when she asked kids to estimate the number of books they'd read during the current year and compare the total with the September figure, they burst out laughing. Every student had lied in the fall—they'd inflated the number of books because, as one student put it, "We'd heard about you. We knew you expected us to be readers."

Donald Murray once told our writer's group, "When my students come in for their conference appointments they do all the talking." We didn't believe him. Bill, another of our members, said, "I have a small grant and I'm going to put a video camera in your office and we'll see about this. Are you game?"

"Sure," said Murray, and the technicians and cameras rolled in. Murray was right. The students did all the talking, because they knew he feasted on their words; with one or two questions he had them talking again, and they usually left knowing more about writing, their subjects, and themselves than when they entered.

We have some input into the book that students are writing about us and need to think more about what is getting into that text.

The Believing Game

In an article titled "The Believing Game," Peter Elbow chose an example from Shakespeare's *Othello* to make his point. There is a moment in the play in which Iago whispers to Othello that Desdemona, his wife, may have been unfaithful. The seed of doubt is sewn, and Othello can't be satisfied until he is absolutely certain that she is faithful. In the end, to remove all doubt, he is forced to kill Desdemona, then weeps at the fruits of his disbelief.

When we teach, belief and disbelief sit side by side. How easy it is to believe that the child is not learning, so we test to find out. Testing provides a number convincing us to what degree the child has or hasn't learned. The number also is assumed to show where the child's learning fits within a much larger population of children across the country.

Margaret Wheatley states that what people need is good solid feedback, not measurement. When we play the believing game with children, we deliberately look for what they know and confirm that knowledge here and now. "I see that you are now making paragraphs. Tell me how you figured that out, right here on your paper." Feedback means noticing intelligently, asking for the child's response, and then confirming his or her process and accuracy.

To play the believing game, we need to
know both the child and the process.

Am I Dressed?

Preoccupied with my upcoming day at school, I drove on automatic pilot along my so familiar route one morning, thinking all the while about books, children, and people to see.

I arrived at the school parking lot and it suddenly struck me that I couldn't recall driving there.

I put my mind in rewind and tried to recall what I'd eaten for breakfast. A blank.

I could feel the blood rush to my face as I looked down at my clothing. Was I dressed? What was I wearing? Was I buttoned in the right places? Did my socks match?

Sometimes we go through life, but life doesn't go through us.

Learning Their Names 13

Before every class I've ever taught in elementary school, middle school, or a university, I've tried to learn the names ahead of time. I put the names in alphabetical order, then memorize them, A though Z. I feel the names on my tongue as I pronounce them, try to picture the child or student behind a name-suggested ethnic background, imagine interesting stories the name might be able to tell.

If I know the names ahead of time, it is much easier to put the face with the name when they walk into that first class saying, "Well, here I am," "Just got here in time," or "Is this the right class?"

Of course, Igor Fedorov is always easier to remember and recognize than Mary Jones. Maybe this goes back to when I was in sixth grade and we studied immigration. I envied the ethnic names of my classmates, and I remember telling my mother, "We aren't from anywhere. Graves isn't from any real country." She did console me with the fact that my first name, Donald, is of Scottish derivation.

The minute I can call a student by her or his first and last name as we make solid eye contact, we each have an existence for the other that we didn't have before.

Behind the Name

Once I know the student's name, I set up another discipline. I find out something distinctive, something unique about what that child knows. Perhaps the child draws well, is a fast runner, always carries a book he is reading, has a sense of humor, has a favorite rock group or ball team, can tell a story.

This discipline takes time. And it means I am deliberately studying my students in the hallway, playground, lunchroom, or library. I carry the names inside my head and slot facts into the blank space opposite them: *Alison plays the piano; Joshua trades cards; Teneesha has a cat; Miguel plays basketball.* These simple facts are placeholders for additional details about the likes, dislikes, and interests of each of my students.

Next, I want to confirm whether my observation is correct. "Teneesha, tell me about your cat." Teneesha may say, "I don't have a cat," or "His name is Mittens, because he has white paws."

*When students sense we know something positive about them,
we establish a firm base for learning more together.*

Family Names

I was on the floor observing kindergartners construct things with blocks. The teacher announced, "Okay, it's time to put your materials away and get ready for music. When I call out your first name, answer with your last name and get in line." Some children needed a slight hint, but a good third couldn't say their surname even then. On the other hand, seven or eight stood and quickly responded, as this boy did, with their full name: "James Michael Callahan."

I've pondered these responses for many years. Clearly, we are becoming an informal society. A child is introduced to his adult neighbors by his father this way: "Timmy, I'd like you to meet our neighbors, Jackson and Samantha." Whenever I hear something like this, I want the father to be more formal, to include a last name. Full names convey ethnicity and generational and matrimonial history. (Of course, names, both first and last, may carry pain as well, the negative connotations of family members who have died or now live elsewhere.)

I didn't appreciate the name Graves until I was much older. It smacked of being English; even worse, I knew both sides of my family had come over on the Mayflower. I wanted a "foreign" last name, one from the middle of Europe, one based in a different language.

There is much for children to learn in growing
to understand both first and last names.

And One to Grow On

I shake my head at all the mistakes I made as a first-year principal. I was only twenty-eight years old, the second-youngest member of the faculty. I knew a fair amount about teaching and learning, but I was both naïve and ignorant about administration. A degree in school administration is no guarantee of maturity or of knowing how to listen. It takes a lifetime of experience to understand the meaning of leadership.

I was a reactionary principal who tried to be bold and decisive. Instead of consulting with a number people and asking for advice, I made my decisions. I was getting paid for being the principal. If I consulted others, it meant I wasn't yet ready for the job. (I was also very aware that I was replacing a much-respected woman and educator.)

One day two teachers complained to me that the lunchroom was a zoo. The noise was insufferable. I issued an insane on-the-spot decree: "From now on, children are not to talk in the lunchroom; they'll have to wait until they go out-side." The complaining teachers were delighted, but I could tell that many other faculty members thought my edict much too extreme. Children need to talk while they are eating. It is the one time in the day when they can be themselves.

Another example. Two months into my administration a teacher told me they needed an opportunity to get to the bathroom during the morning: there was no scheduled break. How had I failed to consider this very basic bodily need?

And there was the time the board decreed that only students who lived more than one mile from the school could be bussed. I calculated precise mileages and determined that the one-mile mark in one direction came directly between two homes about twenty feet from each other. In a curt letter I informed the family just inside the one-mile radius that their children would now have to walk. Again, what ignorance.

When faced with a young principal like me, whose decisions are sometimes difficult to support, make an appointment to talk about learning and teaching.

The Custodian

When I was a principal, my closest ally and the person who taught me the most was Lee Rose, our custodian. If I'd been smarter, I would have realized how essential custodians are to education.

One morning Lee stood in the outer office. He was a patient man, but any time I saw him waiting I ushered him straight in. Lee had insights about kids that I needed to know. (Lee also had a wry sense of humor. "I hate to see Fridays come," he'd say, "because that means Monday is only two days away.") "What's up, Lee?"

"Someone is turning the water off in the urinals in the boy's lavatory. I don't know how they do it, because the turn-off valve is about fourteen feet up from the floor. Some kid is liable to slip going up there and come crashing down onto the cement floor; it could kill him."

"So what do you recommend?"

"I don't know, but I'll think on it."

Several days later Lee returned. "I think I have a solution. You know the backing to the ditto sheets, the purple stuff?" I nodded. "What I aim to do is get up on a ladder and rub that purple ink all over the valve wheel, and next time it's turned off we'll look at all the boys' hands."

Ten days later Lee was again in the outer office. His eyes danced behind a rare grin. "The valve is off. Let's go find the kid." I began with the sixth grade, but had to go all the way down to the third grade before we found a little boy with telltale purple hands.

"Come with us," I said, and we went down to the boys lavatory. "What I want to know is how you were able to turn that valve off?" At first he denied it, but then he leaped for a pipe, swung himself up, stepped on a radiator, grabbed another pipe. I said, "Enough. Come down. Don't you ever do this again. And if you do, we'll know, because this ink is all over it." Lee just smiled. I thanked him for his wisdom.

Be aware of the effect the support staff in your building
have on the emotional and intellectual atmosphere.

The Boy in the Closet

Less than a month after I became principal, the secretary came into my office. "Mr. M. would like to speak with you." I went into the outer office and greeted a tall farmer in bib overhauls.

"What can I do to help you sir?" I asked.

He put out his finger at the end of a long arm and said, "I don't want no teacher putting my son in the closet."

"I'm sure you are mistaken, Mr. M., but I will look into the matter right away."

Mr. M. looked me directly in the eye. "My son tells the truth."

Convinced that Mr. M. was misinformed, I went down to the first-grade classroom. I knew his son's teacher very well. She sat behind me in church. She was a sweet lady with pink cheeks and very white hair. I laughed in embarrassment as I told her why I'd come. "Mr. M. thinks you put his son in the closet."

"I did!" my teacher/friend interrupted. "He was a naughty boy and something had to be done." I was totally taken aback. I couldn't believe this had happened in my building, the action taken by someone I thought I knew.

When I came to my senses I said, "Don't ever do this again. And if things ever get so difficult that you feel the urge to put someone in a closet, you send a note up to get me at once."

I called Mr. M., apologized for the incident, and told him that indeed his son was telling the truth. It wouldn't happen again. As far as I knew it didn't.

Surprises like this one keep us from ever feeling complacent.

Saving the PTA

My PTA board was made up of reasonably well-to-do volunteers who felt comfortable in leadership positions. Mrs. N., an enthusiastic young mother of four children, volunteered to run the cake sale. She rode a motorcycle, barely fit into tight jeans, wore a black jacket, and spoke in a loud voice. Since none of the women on the board enjoyed running the cake sale, they accepted Mrs. N.'s offer, even though it meant she'd attend their meetings.

But Mrs. N. was a worker, and the cake sale went off without a hitch. About a month later, the treasurer reported that she still hadn't received the money from the cake sale and that Mrs. N. hadn't shown up at the recent meeting. The board wanted to take Mrs. N. to court and were about to call the police. I had to do something.

I called Mrs. N. repeatedly, but she never picked up. She knew something was afoot. Finally, I got an automated message that the phone had been disconnected. Since her four children were still attending school, I sent a sealed note home with the eldest. Still no response.

I knew where Mrs. N. lived. I hid my car in a copse of trees across from her home. I knew she was at home, because her laundry was hanging on the clothesline. I also knew that if I knocked she wouldn't come to the door. Two hours later, when her clothes were dry, Mrs. N. came out the back door. I jumped out of my car and raced toward her. "Mrs. N., please listen, but first I need to listen to you."

Her tale of woe poured out. Her husband was a fisherman, and recent storms had resulted in days with no catch. With four children to feed, she'd spent the cake sale money, and her husband still hadn't earned enough money to cover it. What was she to do? We came up with a plan. She got a lien on her motorcycle for $50, I contributed the rest, and I delivered the money to the treasurer. There would be no scandal in the PTA.

So many problems are easily handled if people only talk to each other.

20 Nits

Most textbooks for administrators don't deal with the problem of nits, but in mine the subject would be chapter 1. Nits, or head lice, spread so quickly that two cases can become twenty or more in just a few days. It's a principal's nightmare. The outbreaks usually occur in winter when children put their hats next to each other in cloakrooms or on shelves.

My assistant principal was more experienced in "nit-picking" than I. She could spot nits on the ends of a child's hair just watching her walk by. She also knew the likely "carriers." "Got problems," she said one noon. "That family down on the Neck has lice again. We'd better check all the heads in the school. I'll show you what to look for."

We started with the classrooms in which the family members were students. The children lined up and we parted each child's hair, especially behind the ears. Finding lice was terribly embarrassing for the child in question, because the other children would recoil in mock horror. ("Oooo, she's got bugs.") In our ignorance, especially mine, I'm sure we handled some cases badly.

Then I went to my office and called the parents of the children with nits. When I told one mother, she started to cry. Her daughter had beautifully groomed, long dark-brown hair. "But our home is clean," the mother protested. "You must think we have a filthy house."

I said, "Mrs. C., I think nothing of the sort. It is happening here at school. I'll bring her straight home in my car [this was in the days when staff members could still drive children home], and you can start treatment immediately." I just hoped the mother wouldn't pass her own embarrassment on to her daughter.

If nits pay a visit to your school, chat with the children about the problem before you start examining heads.

Let Students Tell You What They Know

One day when I was observing first graders, I noticed that Scott had used a period at the end of his sentence. Since I hadn't noticed him doing that before, I said, "Scott, I see that you've used a period here. Can you tell me about that?"

"Yes," he said. "You see, I was sliding down the hill, and if I didn't put the period there I'd have gone right through the house." That's one of the best takes on the function of a period I've ever heard.

I've since learned that what I should have asked Scott was, "I see you got that period *in just the right place*. Can you tell me about that?" Children provide better explanations when they hear that what they've done is accurate.

In any case, I want learners of all ages to get very good at explaining how or why they do things. I find they enjoy explaining it to themselves as much as to me. Of course, the question has to be genuine. I really want to know the thinking behind what they've done.

Sometimes they don't really know and are digging to find the reasons behind their performance. Even when their explanations are pure fantasy, I have at least established that there are reasons why things work well. The child who struggles to explain may continue to ask herself, "Yes, how did I manage to get that right?"

It is important for learners to know why things work well.

Traits of Good Teachers

As part of my study on teacher energy, I asked teachers what they valued in their colleagues. They mentioned a list of excellent traits:

- Has a sense of humor.
- Talks about children in specifics and says how he or she learns from them.
- Talks about what doesn't work; asks for help.
- Asks for advice.
- Knows more about you than just your life as a teacher.
- Listens.
- Shares methods and materials.
- Shares books and ideas; talks about interests beyond teaching.
- Has a vision for where he or she is going.
- Is frank and can openly disagree with comfort.
- Explores other points of view while maintaining his or her own point of view.
- Volunteers; steps forward.
- Is more interested in others than centered in himself or herself.
- Is generally filled with energy.

Taking another look at this list, I now see that behind all these admired characteristics is a respect for colleagues who are their own person, who can approve and disapprove with equanimity. I also notice that admired colleagues can laugh at themselves, don't take themselves or the profession too seriously. They share books and ideas but feel free to ask advice of everyone. People just enjoy being around them.

Choose your favorite colleague, and then make two lists.
What makes this person a good colleague? What would
be on the list this colleague makes about you?

A New Teacher Is a Lonely Teacher

It's the rare school that doesn't have a new teacher or two. The teacher turnover rate in the United States is between 12 and 15 percent. If you have at least two years of teaching experience, there is no greater energizer than paying attention to someone who is new in your building.

The first month of teaching can be a very lonely time indeed. Many new teachers are living on their own for the first time, away from the towns in which they were raised, away from college dormitories, fraternities, or sororities. Others have brought a spouse and perhaps children with them to a new apartment or home. More than anything, they need a personal, professional connection.

Helping new teachers need not be time-consuming or complicated. Noticing new teachers is at the top of the list of easy things to do. Notice them in the halls, sit next to them in meetings, talk with them during lunch or recess. Notice what they wear, read, struggle with—*but notice*.

Listen to what they say. Lean forward, make eye contact, really hear their words. Paraphrase what they are saying to see if you have listened carefully enough. If they tell a story, react to it, don't superimpose your own ("You think it's tough now, let me tell you about *my* first week of teaching" is a big turnoff). Instead, honor their words and the feelings behind the words ("So you are feeling as if you've lost control of the class. What do you think is the best thing to do?")

Consult new teachers. At the top of many teachers' list of things that energize them is someone asking what they think. "I mean, they actually thought I might have something to say," said one new teacher in amazement. I know a principal who asks new teachers to share what they are reading at teacher meetings.

New teachers need to be noticed, listened to, and asked
for advice; it energizes them and it energizes us.

Active Listening

Give yourself an assignment. Spend time at home, in the teacher's room, or in the corridor outside your room. Do just one thing, observe and listen. That means you'll have to suspend your usual urge to speak.

Observe two things: the content and the emotion behind the content. Listen for the wish or the "not enough." Here are some examples of what I mean:

1. "I keep getting new students unannounced. They just appear without any papers." I overhear this and think that this person's wish is for more respect from the front office or an acknowledgment of her feelings in the matter.

2. "I've just finished my course at university. One more paper to do and then I'll be home free." It is hard to know if this person is speaking about accomplishment, opening the door to my asking about her course, or just keeping in touch, one friend to another. Another time I might smile and say, "Tell me more." That allows them to elaborate on the true wish.

3. I'm at a meeting. The administrator says with a touch of concern, "We need to prepare the kids for the annual writing prompt. Help them to see how to get started, how to marshal their facts." This time I'm listening for tone that may indicate the wish, which in this case is that the students will do well. Another time I may ask her about the tone.

Begin today to practice active listening for the wishes and feelings behind people's words. This is an essential skill. Of course, we do the same with children.

PART TWO

The Teacher Makes the Difference

It is fashionable to hold the method superior to the teacher. Governments, state departments of education, and even local administrations are convinced that there are surefire approaches to teaching students and scientific evidence to back them up. How easy it is to believe that one method fits all situations. How convenient!

But bypass the teacher and we bypass the brains that know how to translate the method so that it benefits the particular children in the room. There are good approaches to teaching, but they are only as good as the professional who uses them.

We started our year by thinking about children—their names and personalities—becoming acquainted with them. But we need to get to know our colleagues, too, and make use of their expertise. Here are some stories about outstanding teachers, their ideas, their artfulness, and their commitment to children and the profession.

It's the Teacher

The late Jeanne Chall, reading professor at Harvard, and I had our differences over the years. We were good friends arguing back and forth about approaches to research and teaching.

One night I was listening to John Merrow, of National Public Radio, interview Jeanne. John asked, "Tell me, Professor Chall, which would you prefer, a bad teacher with a good method or a good teacher with a bad method?"

"Oh, that's an easy one," she said. "I'd prefer the good teacher with a bad method. That's because in the hands of a good teacher it wouldn't be a bad method any more." I let out a cheer, because I was in complete agreement. The method is never superior to a good teacher.

A wise teacher will always adjust any method to fit the student instead of making the student fit the method.

"This Works Anywhere"

I was in Atlanta, Georgia, attending a National Council for the Teachers of English convention. Nancie Atwell emerged from the writing workshop she had just conducted, her face shining with delight and amazement. "This stuff works anywhere," she exclaimed.

Nancie was at that time already a remarkable teacher in Boothbay Harbor, Maine, but she had never before left Boothbay to teach students in other locations. It is always a delightful shock to learn that children are the same everywhere. When we delight in what they know, show them how their knowing can grow through writing, and then help them notice changes in their voice and learning, students respond.

Nancie brings to her teaching the gifts of absolute presence and the expectation that something wonderful is about to happen. That she doesn't quite know what it might be is precisely what makes learning with her exciting. Students sense when certain answers are expected. From a standards viewpoint this may seem desirable, but it turns teaching and learning into a deadly enterprise. Goals are important, standards are not. A standard suggests the numbing sameness of lockstep learning steps and predigested lesson plans.

Of course, Nancie's excellent teaching doesn't just happen. Nancie reads incessantly, from politics to poetry, and melds the insights she discovers with the interpretations students discover in their own reading. The key word in each instance is *discover*. Nancie often hands a book she has not read to students. "Read this and tell me what you think," she'll say. The student knows that Nancie wants an honest answer about how the book strikes him or her.

Approach each element of curriculum, each life skill, as if you are going to discover something new in the material and in your students.

A Child's Greatest Questions

Children, simply by being children, embody the most important questions. They are a living, feeling text waiting for certain blanks to be filled in.

Does my teacher respect me? Children don't rely on our words, they rely on our facial expression, how close or far away we are, our posture, our gestures, and especially our tone of voice.

Does my teacher think I am smart? Smart is a relative term. Children look to see how we view them in relation to others. Good teachers look carefully and find knowledge unique to each child.

Does my teacher think I can learn? When we set out on a lesson, we must be sure our students know we think they can do it and will help them if they get confused.

*Children feel their way through learning more
than they think their way through it.*

A First-Grade Surprise

I was unprepared for what I encountered in Paula Rogovin's first-grade classroom at the Manhattan New School, in New York City. The children were on the floor making notes about an interview they'd just conducted with the foreman at a nearby high-rise construction site.

For years I've been stressing the importance of interviewing. But this was the first time I'd seen the skill developed in first grade and to a degree far beyond what I'd dreamed possible. The children were learning to read and write through interviewing. Of course, they were also learning how to sequence questions, press adults for information, take notes, and write for publication in their room, the school, and the world.

Virtually all of these students' parents were also interviewed. The children began to understand the roots of their classmates—white, African American, European, Asian, Carribean. One of the most difficult things to teach is point of view. How hard it is for children to put aside their own egocentric opinions and take in the points of view of others. These children took on the feelings of other ethnic groups. Their writing was rich with the language of the people they interviewed.

Discover the wonderful things Paula Rogovin has to say in her books on this subject, *Classroom Interviews* (1998) and *The Research Workshop* (2001).

We need to give children the gift of interview skills so
that they may learn about their world firsthand.

Walking the Walk

Several years ago I was part of a team reviewing a highly regarded suburban school system's program in the teaching of writing. The review required us to observe teachers teaching writing during the month of May and then interview them about their teaching.

One of the gentlemen I observed was teaching second grade. I thought he was an excellent teacher with a genuine regard for children and a full knowledge of the writing process. I learned in my interview that he had been a high school English teacher but that year had elected to try second grade. "I'd like to see what I can do when they are just getting started as writers."

He confided that he'd had a very rough start in September and October, because the parents expected him to circle in red every little word misspelled, each punctuation mark missed. They expected a degree of perfection unrealistic for second graders. "I had the feeling they were worrying about their children getting into Harvard. They even took some of those papers, put in their own red marks, and sent them to the chair of the board of education. Then, in November, I got this off-the-wall idea: the children are publishing, I'm publishing, why not involve the parents too?"

"That's great," I said. "You ought to write an article about that."

"I suppose I could, but I only got a poem and two other short pieces." His face, which had been a bit downcast, suddenly brightened. "You know what? I haven't had a single parent complaint since last November. It never occurred to me why until now."

Ask your students' parents to submit some pieces for publication along with your own and the students.

The Walls Shout

I opened the door to Oyster River Middle School and stopped dead in my tracks. The walls of the hall had been painted over with quotations from the students. Each quote included the author's name and the date it was put up. I had never before seen such a statement of value about language and expression. I asked Linda Rief, an Oyster River English teacher, for the story behind this phenomenon.

"We got a small arts grant to do this. The art teacher taught students to do calligraphy. We set it up so that each quote involved three people, the person who wrote the words, the person who did the calligraphy, and the person who added an illustration." I walked down the hall with Linda and saw work that had been posted over a number of years. "You should see how students bring in their parents and relatives and even revisit the school years later just to look at their quote."

Here are two examples of what these students had to say:

"The Moon of Christmas Eve," by Kerry S.

Its orange glow filled up the night / Shining on the ice. / We stepped onto the path of the moon / And skated into its night.

"Hurricane Gloria's Memory," by Brad P.

The wind whisks. / The clouds dump their trash. / The sticks are battered. / Windows crack / In the harshness of the breeze. / I stop to smell and listen. / There is nothing I can do. / The feeling is powerful. / I try to ride a bike. / Pedaling brings me nowhere. / The eye is peaceful, / Like a frozen rose. / Nearby, / I can sense the ocean / And the undertow.

Post examples of good language: an oral comment
a student has made, a sentence, a poem.

Heaven Without a Ladder

When I was doing research for my book *The Energy to Teach,* Brenda Power told me about a committee in the state of Maine that was trying to understand why certain districts did well on early reading assessments. I was interested: it seemed that most everyone else was fixated on districts that did poorly. At the meeting I attended a woman at the end of my table said, "Excellence doesn't come in a rush; you have to build it over time." Her voice carried some authority, and I made it a point to speak to her during the morning break.

Her name was Virginia Secor. Virginia is the Title I director in four small towns in rural Maine. It's her job to develop staff, improve curriculum, and produce good achievement in all four towns. Over eleven years she has recruited and prepared seven top-level teachers. Ginny is a true pragmatist with an instinct for sound beginnings.

She began with writing, since no one was really teaching writing. "I began with first grade and had my team read student papers. We came up with our own criteria for deciding which pieces worked and which didn't. We decided what we needed to do to get better writing, but—and this is the key—we used our own children's work as the guide to excellence. We hold our workshops in a different building in one of the four towns each time. Teachers arrive an hour early to get the run of the school. It's always open house, and teachers can see how others are approaching reading, writing, or any other aspect of curriculum."

"You have your own way of doing a very wonderful thing. How do you explain that?" I asked.

She replied, "When I was in parochial school, I did the best drawing depicting the concept of going to heaven. The nun said I'd get a blue ribbon if I just put a ladder into the picture. I said, 'No, I like mine the way it is,' and I've been comfortable with being different all my life."

Stand by the things you do well, be true
to your own vision of excellence.

There Is Excellence Within Us All

I've known Shelley Harwayne for nearly twenty-one years. What a fascinating journey she has taken from teaching in Brooklyn to working at Columbia to establishing the Manhattan New School to becoming a district superintendent in New York City. And those are only the smallest fraction of her accomplishments.

I've always been impressed with her uncompromising integrity regarding children and their learning. She once had one of her teachers removed from the building. "This teacher is not kind to children, she must go," she told the powers that be. Kindness to children is Shelley's first priority.

It seemed every teacher at the fledgling Manhattan New School had a different method of teaching. Shelley seemed to delight in the uniqueness of each member of her staff, from the custodian to the secretary to every individual teacher. She saw something unique in them that cried out to be developed, something worth sharing with the world, and many of her teachers have gone on to write and publish books of their own. If all the members of a staff feel that the standard for excellence exists within them, they will pass on this same attitude to the children they teach. After one of my visits I wrote back to Shelley, "I have never seen such intelligent love in a staff."

Shelley deliberately gets her paperwork out of the way each morning before the children and faculty arrive. After that, she is rarely in her office; she's on the move, meeting children, teachers, and parents. She calls each of 550 children by name, talks about their writing, the books they are reading. One day she stopped a student: "Sing 'Danny Boy' for Mr. Graves." The child's face lit up, as did mine, and what a treat it was to hear such lovely music!

Go to a colleague today and remind her of a unique
trait she has, compliment him on his special talent,
talk about its beauty and contribution.

How to Get Good Voice into Reports

Lucy Calkins is a pragmatist. She sees when things work and when they don't. After observing children write reports, she realized that the old ways of teaching report writing produced poor results. She recommended changes that turned my head around, and I've been following her advice ever since.

"First," she said, "the assigned reports are too long. They encourage children to copy references and more or less think quality is associated with length rather than good thinking. When they are first learning, maybe a page and a half is long enough." I assigned twelve-page reports to my seventh graders, and I remember quite clearly the very poor quality of their writing.

"The next issue," Lucy went on, "is how to help students get their voice into the text, to really sound like they have control of the information."

"And how do you do that?" I asked.

"Through interviews. After children have taken their notes, ask them to tell you what they found out; they should get used to feeling the subject on their tongue. When they feel ready they should do a fast draft, right off the top of their head, so that their voice controls the information. Then they can use their notes to put in details they might have missed."

When I saw the quality of her students' writing I knew she was right. With reports a page and a half long, students can do much more revising and stop trying to impress readers with content that isn't a part of them.

The old ways aren't necessarily the best ways.

Miss Fitch

Miss Fitch used flies to cast for rainbow trout, knew her birds and anything else in the flora-and-fauna world. She was my high school biology teacher. I knew she was a good teacher, and everyone else did too. As seniors we dedicated our high school yearbook to her, even though we had taken biology in our sophomore year. As a teacher myself for the past fifty years or so, I've tried to figure out what she did that made her so special.

She wanted us all to fall in love with biology. That meant she had to know both her students and the subject. Within each student lay the key that would release his or her love of biology. But maybe it was the other way around. Maybe we loved Miss Fitch, and we deliberately found a way to tell her personal things (I wanted to hybridize gladiolus, for example) that connected us to biology.

I remember as if it were yesterday the lesson she taught on birds in our area. I can still see her pointing to the chart and identifying the scarlet tanager, the cardinal, and rose-breasted grosbeak. The minute I got home from school that day I headed out to the brush behind our home to spot birds. I even identified several from the chart. I've been identifying birds ever since.

Good teachers set conditions that help students
fall in love with their subjects.

A Rude Awakening

I was on a tour of a school in a Chicago suburb. Eventually, I made my way down to a first-grade classroom. The teacher knew I was coming: the district administration wanted me to watch her writing lesson.

The teacher was energetic but precise. "Who will share with the class today?" A dozen hands went up. But each child stood at attention by his or her desk when speaking. The desks were one behind the other, row upon row. There seemed to be a system of behavior for each classroom routine: *pay attention, stand up, no talking out of turn, be respectful, thank you, no thank you.* The teacher appeared to be close to retirement age. "Old school, " I thought.

"It is now time to write. You know what to do. Get busy. Mr. Graves will be moving about the room. He may ask you some questions." The class dug into their writing without delay. I fully expected the results to be formulaic, many pieces on the same topic, each using the same way of getting into the text.

I approached a child. She was writing an interesting piece about her cat, in well-developed sentences using words fully spelled. I crossed the room to a boy who was writing about the Chicago Bulls and Michael Jordan. He was using an extraordinary range of conventions for a first grader. Child after child wrote in a unique voice, and a wide range of topics was evident.

My prejudice was unmasked. Seeing the room layout and the manner of the teacher, I had expected a controlled conformity. Instead, this wonderful teacher used the positive aspects of predictability in a way that resulted in highly individual texts of great quality.

The bottom line is a strong student voice in a high-quality text; there are many ways to get there.

Encouragement Breeds Success

I was fifteen and had just read Irving Stone's biography of Jack London, who lived a rough life, traveled on his own, and was a self-made man. I yearned to be a writer like London.

My English teacher that year, Mrs. Florence Dower, was a rebel. We never knew what she would say or do next. To make a point she might jump up on her desk. The first day she raced to the window, lifted the sash, turned on a dime, and said, "Thought I might jump, didn't you?" But she loved to teach English, and when she read aloud, language jumped from her tongue in inspiration. She especially loved Keats and Shelley, and we did because she did. But she could just as easily go after a student she'd decided was lazy or who was unsympathetic to the beauty of the language.

I steeled my courage and approached her. "Mrs. Dower, what does it take to be a writer? I'd like to be one." She studied my face for a minute, perhaps checking to see how serious I might be.

"Write and rewrite," she said, "We'll begin tonight." She gave me an assignment to write about Jack London. How I worked to make sure the language was tight, the points well made. I brought it in the next day. She went to work, putting comments and questions here, there, and everywhere, and said, "Do it again." We did this for the next two weeks, and then I lost interest. The discipline was too much for me.

What I remember, though, is that Mrs. Dower never laughed or made a nasty comment. My prior performance in class hadn't been that laudable, but she took me at my word and set me to work.

We need to honor any initiative or dream a student might have.

A Teacher's Influence

We have always known that outstanding teachers have far-reaching influence, but that influence has rarely been traced by researchers. A Harvard research team (Pedersen et al. 1978) setting out to study the stability of IQs in Montreal, Canada, schools discovered the effect of one teacher by accident. They noted that in one low socioeconomic neighborhood the IQs of the children in one particular room in one particular school were significantly higher and remained high and stable throughout the children's school careers. The team switched gears.

They learned not only that the children from Miss A.'s room went on to be outstanding students but that they became active in their communities as well. They traced as many of these children as they could and interviewed them as adults. Her former students spoke of Miss A. as if they'd just left her class yesterday. She was a powerful motivating force, helping children believe in themselves, support one another, and develop a social conscience.

But Miss A.'s influence went well beyond the children she had in class. When the team interviewed others from the same time period they testified that they'd had Miss A. when in fact they only attended the school. Her influence throughout the school was that pervasive.

All of us can remember one outstanding teacher who not only affected her own students but every student in the school. The standard of human excellence lives on even when the particular vessel is gone.

When children or students come back to visit your classroom, ask them what they remember most about when they were with you.

"They Care What I Think!"

A friend in Oregon said, "I was quite surprised when one day in a meeting someone asked me how I would handle the grouping of our very large fifth grade next year. What surprised me was the energy I felt from being looked on as a respected professional colleague."

A new teacher told me that her principal asked her to talk to the faculty about a professional book she was reading. In sharing the book, she felt she was introducing herself to the faculty as well. "I was being asked for my professional opinion."

Professional respect is a true energizer.

"We Can Do That"

39

"Where were you yesterday, Mrs. Giacobbe?" one of her first graders asked.

"I went down to Belmont, Massachusetts, to observe a teacher and some children while they were writing. Let me show you what they were doing." Mary Ellen told her students about how the children in Belmont were using "invented spelling." "See, you don't have to spell the words perfectly the first time. You can spell it like it sounds, like this word, *Halloween*."

"You mean you had to go all the way to Belmont to learn how to do that?" one child asked, slightly insulted. A murmur rustled through the group. Another child said, "We already know how to do that."

"Okay then, if you are so sure you know how, take your papers this morning and show me."

And from that day on, the children in Mary Ellen's room expanded their writing to include a broader range of topics through invented spelling. They'd felt confined by having to write about the assigned topic of the day using words already spelled for them on the board or on a handout.

At every turn, in every situation, we must look for
ways for children to become more independent.

Starting from Scratch

Russell was getting ready to teach fifth grade in an Armed Forces School overseas. The principal was at a loss over this particular class; the students had already driven two previous teachers to resign. Russell said, "I want to start this class my way, which means no interruptions for at least a week." The principal readily agreed.

When the fifth graders arrived in the room they were astonished to find all the books, tables, chairs, materials, etc., in a heap in the center. Russell was seated on the floor at the far end. He beckoned the children to sit in a circle around him.

"We're going to set this room up the way we want it to work, but first we're going to talk about learning and what interests you. We have all the time we need, because no one is going to bother us while we make this our place, our room." The stunned children were silent at first, not knowing whether to take him seriously.

"Animals," said one, "I want to learn about all kinds of animals."

"Whales," said another.

"How people dress in other countries."

They spent the morning talking about interesting things to learn. A vision began to grow about learning interesting things.

"What about all that stuff in the middle of the room?" a child asked.

"Oh, that. Well, we're going to decide how the room gets set up based on what we want to learn." They spent the rest of the day deciding where to put desks, tables, books, and equipment. Many schemes were tried, as Russell taught them how to discuss and plan. Everyone was involved both in the decision making and in picking up and moving things into place. Russell got a good picture of the leadership qualities and skills of these students, and the children were able to expend their energy productively.

The more children are invested in designing curriculum and the classroom, the more they will be engaged in active learning.

Freddy

A pivotal moment occurred in my teaching years ago that I first started to write in narrative form. The narrative wasn't working so I switched to writing it as a poem. In fact, the poem rests in the front of my book, *The Energy to Teach.*

Freddy

Until that moment, ferret-faced Freddy
Ruined my days. Eggs sat cold
On my morning plate, the weather
Cloudy and grey, and
When I turned out the light I heard
Him laugh, "I wasn't doin'
Nothing, Mr. Graves."

But on that day
When with eyes
Lit by new fire he asked,
"Did you know
Humpback pods create
A new song each year?" Something
Jumped between us.

We each built new lives on
That simple question; Freddy
Followed his whales and I've
Been looking for what kids know
Ever since.

There are turning points in our careers
that we can recall with great profit.

PART THREE

Family Matters

One day one of my students ran into me in the supermarket. He looked at the items in my basket, then looked up with a quizzical expression that said, So you eat food too? Children forget that we have lives apart from the classroom. And maybe we forget that we grew up within families and that we have families of our own right now. We are never just teachers.

The following stories from my and my daughters' lives as children within a family may trigger some of yours. Things in your own background explain why you teach as you do today.

Telling Stories

My Uncle Reg was quite a teller of stories. Whenever he visited, we'd beg to hear them. How he'd relish telling about, for example, the snakes in North Carolina, where he worked during the winter. I admired his ability to spin a tale, and I sensed the power storytellers have over their audience.

One day Dad sent me up to the gas station to get him a can of Prince Albert tobacco for his pipe. He wrote me a note to give to Mrs. Bradley, the proprietor. "What's new, Donald?" Mrs. Bradley asked. I was six years old and didn't want to disappoint a woman with white hair and pink cheeks who looked as though she had just stepped out of the pages of a Mother Goose book.

"My Dad is going to work for the WPA."

"Oh, really?"

"Yes, he's going to start Monday."

Several days later Dad confronted me. The Works Progress Administration offered jobs to men who were out of work, and he was a very visibly employed school principal. I'd seen the WPA men working on the highway with picks and shovel, the sun catching the sweat on their arms, and I'd thought, "I wish my dad did that." Hence my fabrication. I didn't explain the workings of my mind to Dad, though; I just looked down in embarrassment.

About two weeks later I volunteered to Mrs. Bradley that we were going on a two-day overnight boat trip. (We didn't own a boat, and Dad had no plans to rent one.) Again, Dad confronted me. "Donald, if you keep telling stories, people aren't going to believe you when you have a true story to tell."

Why did I tell those stories? Did I want to command an audience like my Uncle Reg? Mrs. Bradley was certainly a good listener, and maybe I wanted to impress her. Or perhaps my stories were unfulfilled wishes. If I said it, maybe it would really happen.

Listen for the wish behind the story.

Growing Pains

For the longest time I was the smallest boy in my class. My nickname was Rabbit, because I was so small and had big ears. I didn't start growing until I was a sophomore in high school and was still growing—three inches!—during my freshman year of college. Consequently, I have always thought of myself as being below average height and a very late bloomer. I published my first book when I was fifty-two, I ran my first half marathon at sixty-eight.

I wrote the following poem in *Baseball, Snakes, and Summer Squash* (1995) to vent the feelings of my younger years:

Growing Pains

When we line up for gym,
I'm the last in line.
Even Tommy Crawford next to me
Is an inch taller.
"Rabbits are always small,"
He says with a grin.

Mother says, "It's time
You saw a doctor."

"He's no smaller than me
When I was his age,"
My father argues.

"We've waited long enough.
We're going Monday."

I tell Jimmy I'm going
To the doctor.
He says, "They'll pull
Your pants down, you know."

Dr. Seymour has a pretty nurse,
And I know she'll be standing
There when he pulls my pants down.

She smiles, "Come right
This way, Donald."

"Not growin' huh,"
Says Dr. Seymour.
"We'll see about that."
The nurse smiles
And stands there
Holding a clipboard
With some papers on it.

"Put out your arms,
Straight in front
Of you like this."
Dr. Seymour has a tape,
And he measures all my bones—
Arms, legs, and feet.
"No worries here, Donald.
You'll grow, no doubt about it.
Go play baseball."
I smile at the nurse.

Spend some time observing the smallest children in your class today.

Busy Hands Make Good Thinking

One of the regular chores my brother and I had to endure was drying the dishes. Mother stood at the sink scrubbing the dishes in hot, soapy water. Either my brother or I stood next to her, taking the dishes out of the drainer one by one and drying them. When I was sixty-four, in the middle of writing a poem on this subject, it struck me that we didn't really need to dry the dishes. They'd have dried just standing there for a half hour or so.

But Mother's real objective was daily conversations with her sons about work, life, money, and moral issues. She asked about how we spent our days, what our goals were, what sports we liked to play, whatever she wanted to know. It was a family version of the ancient community practice of scrubbing clothes at the river and getting caught up on the latest gossip.

There's nothing like good conversation while our hands are busy doing something else. We're not staring at each other; the talk flows easily while we look down at our work. A study of very young children working on crafts showed that their language and ideas were richest when they were doing something with their hands.

I've watched teachers sitting next to a child who is struggling with a text. They don't address the child's inability to write. Rather, they do some writing themselves, chatting back and forth with the child about writing, reading, whatever. No longer going it alone, the child is soon into his writing, his mind more relaxed and able to focus.

In a community of learners, busy hands are connected to better work.
Isolation is broken, conversation flourishes, work improves.

Budget Envelopes

Mother lectured about finances: "Don't be like your father. Budget, save for what you want, and think twice about spending." Mother gave us the impression that at any moment disaster would strike and, thanks to Dad's lack of foresight, we wouldn't have any money.

Dad was generous to a fault. He was constantly giving money to people who needed it. When we were older, my brother and I would joke that he had "the fastest wallet in the East." Dad constantly worried about the welfare of his boys. I remember the day he decided his sons should have real leather baseball mitts. We strode into Sears and bought the gloves, and when we got home Mother asked him, "You didn't spend the food money, did you?" Of course, he had. He cared more about playing baseball than eating.

When I was about ten Mother instituted a new system of handling the family's money. She bought budget envelopes. She'd cash Dad's check, then slot the money into different envelopes: food, rent, telephone, electricity, clothes. She gave Dad an allowance. Of course, Dad would run through his funds a little too quickly, and Mother made a little ceremony of taking the funds he "desperately" needed from the food or church envelope.

My brother and I were fascinated. George got Mother's old envelopes, and I actually bought new ones for myself. Labeling them *toys, church, savings, sports, games,* we split our twenty-five cent allowance between them. Sometimes we'd pool our sports envelopes if we wanted something we both would use, like a new baseball.

George and I still each use a modified "envelope" system to keep careful track of our finances. George went on to be vice president of Citizens Bank of New England. Both of us carry no monthly indebtedness. It isn't that we fear being in debt; rather we've learned how to manage our money so that it's there when our families and the less blessed need it.

For better or worse, teaching within the family is always the most powerful teaching and has the greatest long-term effect.

Sibling Rivalry

When we lived in the city, not much was made of Halloween; sometimes we'd buy a cheap mask and wear it to school. But in East Greenwich, Rhode Island, Halloween was something special. We appeared at the school in our afterthought masks to find hundreds of kids in elaborate costumes standing on the playground. The kids with the best costumes received a prize. One of the winners was a boy with a huge frame on his shoulders covered by a ghoulish sheet. I made a mental note.

The next year I asked Mother if I could design my own costume. She readily agreed: she'd have one less to worry about. I spent my full allowance of twenty-five cents on a plastic pumpkin, poked a hole in either side, put a ribbon of thin cloth through one side and out the other, then tied the two ends under my chin so the pumpkin rested on my head. I put a flashlight inside the pumpkin so the light shone through the eyes and mouth, and prayed that the battery would last. Mother helped me put a big sheet around the pumpkin head, over my shoulders, and down to the ground. I cut two tiny slits so that I'd be able to navigate.

When I got to school, there were two hundred kids in costume. I turned on the flashlight and tried to make myself obvious to the judges. A woman judge came over, took me by the arm, and ushered me into the winner's circle. My prize was a small pocketknife with a yellow casing.

My brother George, who was two years younger, usually beat me at cards, Parcheesi, Monopoly, shooting baskets, baseball. When I displayed my prize at home, he exploded. Why hadn't Mom and Dad designed him a costume better than mine? I kept quiet and enjoyed his anguish, as Mom and Dad promised him that next year he'd be a winner, just wait and see.

Sibling rivalry within families can be fierce and often shapes the direction lives take. Don't add to it by comparing children in the same family.

Family Chores

Mom and Dad were hard workers, and they wanted to pass on that ethic to their sons. That meant we had daily chores to complete: I had to feed the dog, dry dishes, keep my room neat, and mow the lawn. We received (in the early forties) an allowance of about twenty-five cents a week.

As part of our contribution to the World War II effort, we took in as boarders a couple of the men who were building Quonset Naval Base. One of my jobs was to make their beds. Mother, being a nurse, knew all about making beds, and she lectured me on how to do it—but made sure to do so within the context of the process. There was only one way: keep it smooth and tucked in and use hospital corners so the sheets would never pull out. I can see her now snapping the corners as she showed me how.

Dad plunged into work at high speed, looking neither left nor right. He didn't talk about work. He did it. When it came to weeding the garden, one of my most hated chores, we'd start together and within fifteen minutes Dad would have already finished the row. He had strong fingers that ripped their way through the stubborn weeds. I dreamed my way through the row thinking of anything but what I was doing. Dad said about his own father, "People say that my dad never walked when he could run as he delivered milk from his farm." I always felt slow when working next to Dad. I wondered if I'd ever be a good worker.

One day our next-door neighbor hired me to mow the lawn, rake leaves, and clear the ground between the bushes. I started at eight and rang her bell at eleven. "I'm finished, Mrs. H." The look of surprise on her face as she went out and inspected what I had done frightened me. "I simply can't believe you've done this so well and so quickly," she said.

Sometimes children and even adults need a different venue to show what they can do. They need a fresh start with no comparisons.

Roots

In sixth grade my teacher, Miss Fortin, began a unit on immigration. She called out country after country and asked us to put up our hand when we heard our place of origin.

"Italy." Amadeo Franzone's, Eddie Denise's, Bernice Maneiro's, and five other hands went up. (We lived in Rhode Island, where many Italians had emigrated.) As their hands waved in the air, I began to ponder my own identity. I didn't really come from any other country.

"Sweden." David Nichols, Elisabeth Lindberg, Bobby Anderson, and Terry Dahlquist raised their hand. I could feel the heat building within me. What was I? Where was I from? Who was I? I tried to think back through the generations in my family.

"Ireland." Agnes Scully, Roy Corr, and Jane Mullen. By now only a few children hadn't yet put their hand up.

"France." Two hands. "Germany." One. There I was, the only kid without his hand up. As far as back as I could think, all of our family was from the United States.

"Hah, he's not from anywhere," said Bobby Anderson, in a voice everyone could hear.

Miss Fortin tried to help me. "Maybe it's England," she said with encouragement. What a boring place, I thought. They just speak English.

I went home for lunch and shouted at Mother, "We aren't from anywhere!" She tried to explain that both sides of our family had come over on the Mayflower. I wanted none of that nonsense.

The sense of identity in children is very much attached to a language or country. It is important for us to help them have a sense of roots.

Dreams

Between the ages of nine and seventeen I recall hearing so often and so clearly my mother saying, "The trouble with you, Donald, is that you never finish anything." She was right.

I had big dreams and went after them. I tried to build model airplanes but somehow I could never put them together right. The uncompleted pieces lay abandoned on my desktop. I wanted my own garden of gladiolus, even wanted to breed new varieties as my father did. I'd turn over the sod, shake it out, make neat rows, plant the glads, but I failed to weed what I'd planted. I wanted to learn to play the drums, but I couldn't feel the beat. I got a job selling magazines door to door: I'd make so much money I'd need to hire others to help me! But I hated ringing doorbells and asking people to buy *Liberty* or *True Story*. In seventh grade Albie Underwood and I decided to write a book about Jim Brady and the Marines, a book other kids our age would enjoy. It would be a best seller. We wrote one chapter and lost interest.

And this is just the short list. I had dreams galore but not the will or ability to see them through. I'd begin to do chores, then get to dreaming and forget what I had started.

My parents were sitting in the audience when I stood on the stage of the Hilton Hotel accepting the David H. Russell Award for excellence in research. I pointed to them and said, "I finished it. Thank you."

Dreams are often larger than the ability of the person to accomplish them, but that doesn't matter. The ability to dream must never be stifled. Some day the dream will fit the person.

Deep Play

During World War II my friends and I, twelve and thirteen years old, thought we should prepare for our own participation in case it didn't end before we could join a branch of the service. We decided to simulate a B-17 bombing mission.

I had one large refrigerator box. My friends found three other boxes. From them and a kit I'd sent away for that contained a control panel, left and right rudder pedals, and a steering wheel (all made of cardboard) we managed to construct a wingless B-17 Flying Fortress in my basement. That took the good part of a weekend. As we built the bomber, we talked about where in Germany we should simulate the mission. I'd read that Dusseldorf had ball-bearing factories, so that became our target. We assigned parts: pilot, copilot, navigator, waist gunner, tail gunner, and top bubble gunner. We role-played a briefing of what to expect and why. This was serious business; we were going to carry out our mission in real time, make it take as long as the real thing.

Our navigator charted the distance, figured the air speed, and told us it would take four hours to get to the target and back. Prepared with sandwiches, we took off from an airfield in England, flew to our target, fought off fire from Messerchmitt 109s, dropped our bombs, and returned—never leaving our boxes for four hours. (I felt for the tail gunner, cramped in a very small space for that length of time!) That was our one and only mission. But we learned lots about planning, flight simulation, and the excitement and boredom of war. We'd done our best in preparing for our future roles.

Deep play has an important role in the developing lives of children. I suspect it is closely tired with long-range thinking. Children need to experience their own and their friends' imaginations, apart from adults, apart from computer games. They need sustained time in which to carry detailed experiences to a successful conclusion.

We must find ways to become acquainted with and demonstrate that we value the deep play of our students.

When Someone Dies

When I was eight years old, my mother lost a full-term baby. Mother was a nurse and had taken my brother and me through the pregnancy step by step, explaining the various phases of growth, letting us feel the baby kick, answering our questions. Then, at the very end of her term, Mother nearly bled to death from a placenta previa, and she—and we—lost the baby. Not only that, my mother and her no-nonsense explanations were taken away from us for the two weeks of her hospitalization. Our two grandmothers handled the problem of emotional loss by hard work: "We have to do all that we can to help your father," one advised. Poor Dad was torn between work, running to the hospital, and caring for his sons. He wasn't used to explaining emotional situations, least of all death. He was so happy he hadn't lost his wife, we our mother, that the notion of dealing with the loss to the family of a full-term fetus never came up.

When I wrote a fuller account of this experience for my 1998 collection of stories *How to Catch a Shark,* I began to sob as all the loss, anger, and bewilderment of that time hit me full force.

As teachers we may never know some of the awful struggles our students have had to endure. Children who have suffered emotional trauma need to be listened to at length by adults who have earned their trust. There is no formula for dealing with it quickly and effectively. In some cases professional help is needed.

Getting Mad

One day our daughter Alyce came home from school quite upset. She was nine years old and in the third grade. Her teacher had berated another child, an old-fashioned dressing down meant to humiliate the little boy. What the teacher said to the boy, Alyce took unto herself. She felt what the boy felt. I imagine there were many other children who felt as Alyce did. A blast like that overheard by an entire class sends out lots of shock waves.

Of course, I have berated students too. Certain students knew my buttons, knew just what to do or say to get my goat. Sure enough, I'd explode. Perhaps the class enjoyed seeing me lose my cool. I'm only human.

It's also human to apologize (though I haven't always done it). But when I had returned to an even keel and reflected on my behavior, I usually explained that what I had done wasn't right.

We all get angry at times, but we need to apologize
and say why it was wrong for us to have done so.

Lessons from a Daughter

I tried to teach our younger daughter to drive. Instead, *she* taught *me* how to teach her to drive.

Invariably, whenever I was in a rush to get to the university, Laura spotted her opportunity: "Move over, Dad, I need practice."

She backed down our twisted driveway, stalling several times, and finally we headed down the street. Our car had a standard transmission, and she hadn't yet gotten the feel of the transition from the clutch to the gas pedal. I tried to hold my exasperation at the lost time in check. In three tenths of a mile we reached the stop sign signaling a slightly more traveled country road.

Laura saw a car coming a quarter mile down the road and decided to wait. I writhed with impatience. As she carefully checked left and right, another car loomed into view. Again, she didn't move. I started to breath heavily. After a third car started around the bend and she still wasn't moving, I said, "Laura, please, you can go now. You can go when cars are that far away."

"Listen, Dad, you've been driving for thirty-seven years. You're telling me when you would go. I've only been driving for three weeks, and if you don't want to get ploughed you'll have to go at my speed."

How many times do we try to teach our students
at the speed of our experience rather than theirs?

A Relaxed Day

I spent a year in Scotland, writing my first book. Our daughter, Laura, then thirteen, attended the schools in the nearby town of North Berwick. Her day was long: she left home in the dark at seven a.m. and didn't return on the bus until four-thirty in the dark afternoon. She carried six major subjects, including three sciences. But when she walked in the door she was relaxed and happy.

Although her day was long and her classes were challenging and required good preparation, her schedule was well paced. She had a full hour for lunch, which included a relaxed time in which to play cricket, run, or just read a book. And extracurricular activities, like singing, dancing, and sports, were interspersed between classes rather than piled up after school as they are in the United States.

Laura made many good girlfriends—as many as fourteen—who regularly visited our home, as she visited theirs, and with whom she enjoyed parties and sleepovers. But there was little of the stressful pairing off of girls and boys. All the children wore a school uniform, to which they could add their own small individual touches, so there were no morning struggles about what she should wear.

Although Laura had homework, she spent more time reading books for pleasure during that one year in Scotland than at any time in her school years in the States.

When we returned to the States and Laura went through her pressure-filled ninth-grade days, eight-thirty to two-fifteen, she was ready to put her fist through the wall because the tension was so great. There was little time to converse, eat, reflect, read, and above all learn.

We need to rethink the length and depth of our school days in
order to allow greater learning on the part of our children.

Love in Bloom

When I give talks, I often ask the audience, "How many of you remember being in love in elementary school?" Eighty to 90 percent of the group raise their hand. Next, "How many of you remember the name of the person you were in love with?" About 75 percent of the hands stay up. There is nothing quite like a first love in elementary school. It is such a wonderful surprise and shock to the system. I wrote a poem about my first love in fourth grade, "Elisabeth" (*Baseball, Snakes, and Summer Squash*, 1995).

Elisabeth

A clump of boys
From fourth grade
Stand on the playground
Not speaking about
Much of anything at all
Until talk of love and girls
Sneaks in from the edges
Of somewhere.

"I love Elisabeth Lindberg,"
I say quickly, thinking
My early statement might
Get me first dibs.

"So do I," says Jimmy.
"Me too," interrupts Robert.

"I've loved her ever since
First grade," argues Nicky.
"No, no, she knows I love her,"
Shouts Paul, "I told her."
"You did!" we chorus.
"What did she say?"
"Nothing."

We sigh our relief
Like the aaaaaah
Of a Pepsi
On a hot summer day.
And every once
In a while we bunch
Again on the playground
And speak of Elisabeth
As if our talk
Makes love more possible.

Love is everywhere in classrooms. Have a good time observing
at least five children who show evidence of being in love.

PART FOUR

Learning from Children

I*t is easy to say, "We learn from the children." The words may come easily, but the practice comes hard. We know what we want to teach, but there are so many children we have to reach that it is hard for us to read each heart and maintain a classroom that is emotionally healthy for everyone. Perhaps now, approximately three months into the school year, it's time to consider individual children and all the ways we might come to know them. The first snow has fallen if we live in the north. We and our students are anticipating the holidays. Seasonal music is in the air. Window displays and commercials distract us. But we look up from our books and curriculum guides and attempt to see our children more clearly.*

Some children are perplexing: we simply don't know how to help them. About these children we consult our colleagues, present the evidence, ask them what they hear in the details. But there are always other children who are quiet, retiring, who don't want to be seen. They spend their lives being part of the woodwork. They don't bother us, and we sometimes find ourselves saying, "Thank heaven for good little Mary." We need to become active observers of all our students.

The Face of Expectation

I am in Harrisburg, Pennsylvania, in a public television studio. Eighty teachers surround Mary Ellen Giacobbe, who is going to demonstrate the teaching of writing with a dozen fourth graders.

"Good morning, children," beams Mary Ellen. "I'm sure you have read many interesting books. Tell me about some of them." She leans toward the children in expectation. But after a good minute and a half their faces are as blank as when she entered. No one responds.

She makes another request. "You must have been writing about many topics. Tell me about some of those topics." Again she leans forward, her face full of expectation. Again no one responds. I shift in my seat. The audience of teachers rustles nervously: why aren't the children responding?

But Mary Ellen displays no outward tension and continues to smile and wait. Finally, one boy, Ralph, raises his hand. "Yes, Ralph."

"I love my father."

"That's wonderful, Ralph. Can you tell me about it?"

"My Dad was in an accident. A truck hit his car."

Ralph has broken the ice. Other children begin talking about things that have happened to them. A Korean girl tells about not knowing English so she can't tell the bus driver where she lives. Soon all the children are writing and sharing.

A teacher who leans in with the face of expectation,
her whole body listening, is a gift to children.

The Smallest One

I remember the day I accompanied a little African American boy to his home. He had been in a fight; his clothes were slightly torn, and he had bruise on his face. Since this was not his first fight, I wanted to see whether his family could shed any light on the situation. I knocked and his mother, Mrs. R., opened the door. She invited me in and I asked quite seriously, "Do you have any idea why Anthony gets into so many fights?" She looked at me in utter bewilderment, almost pity.

"He's the smallest one. That's all." Simple fact. Simple truth. How could I have forgotten what it was like being the smallest person in my elementary school? Here's the first stanza of the poem I wrote about my own experience:

The Bully

Bobby Nelson is the toughest kid in our class.
I am the smallest.
His hoarse voice finds me every day
On the way to school and home again.
"Hey, Rabbit, whatcha doin?"
He walks next to me,
Throws his elbow into my ribs
And edges me to the curb
Hoping I'll take a swing at him.
I tried once and he flipped
Me like a toy dog.

*Choose the two smallest children in the class and
look at the school day through their eyes.*

58 Pets

It's difficult to appreciate fully the bond that exists between children and pets. I don't mean just dogs and cats but the larger world of snakes, gerbils, squirrels, chipmunks, birds, horses, grasshoppers, praying mantises, deer, foxes, badgers, etc.

Children have a nurturing side, a side that feeds, plays with, observes, and grows attached to the pets they care for. Along with the caring there is tenderness and a feeling of friendship. They assign moods and attitudes to them. (Of course, not all children react like this. Some want to have power over the pet, to the point of doing cruel things. Such behavior could be a red flag for other personality problems.)

It is in connection with pets that children often encounter death for the first time. Depending on how old a child is, the death of a pet can be quite traumatic. Very young children see death as reversible, but by the age of nine or ten children begin to see death as the end of relationship. One of the most traumatic deaths I've had to deal with was that of my dog, Rags, when I was ten years old. Rags had just been hit by a car, and mother could tell her back was broken. The entire family was crying. Here are the last two stanzas of a poem, "The Accident" (in *Baseball, Snakes, and Summer Squash,* 1995), I wrote about it:

The vet says, "She can live
But she'll never walk again."
We talk it over, say goodbye
To Rags, and she licks my hand
Through the wire cage
For the last time.
I can't stop crying.

The next day I take
My mother's evening purse

With jewels on the outside,
Collect all Rags' hair
From the rug, in the corners
Of the room, and under the
    couch,
Rub it under my nose, sniff
It, cry some more
And put the purse
Under some papers
In my desk drawer.

Some of children's deepest feelings arise in relation
to acquiring, caring for, and losing pets.

Andy

Andy emerged from the mass of faces in December of my first year of teaching. I was too inexperienced to spot what should have been obvious. Whenever I looked at him, his eyes darted to the side or down to his desk. He wore trousers that were much too large for him and at times exuded a distinctive odor. There were shiny, red marks on his arms that could have been burns.

This was long before the days when schools reported problems of child abuse to the authorities. We simply called his mother. When she arrived, she said, "If he gives you any trouble, just clout him side the head like this." With that she struck him a glancing blow. Andy knew she was going to hit him and had moved his head to the side. We raised the question of the red marks that looked like burns. "He's always playing with matches; that's probably where he got them."

Quite often things would be missing from my room. I didn't want to suspect Andy, but I did. And what about the rumors that Andy set fires? I worried but didn't know what to do. Andy was intelligent and wrote reasonably well, but I didn't know how to bring him into our fragile classroom community. The children kept him at the social edge, and he knew less about becoming a class member than I knew about how to help him do so.

I'd like to think that today I'd know what to do. But there are always children who are just beyond our reach emotionally.

Emotional barriers are far more complicated
than instructional problems.

"I Think I Know How I Write"

We were in the middle of our research into children's writing in Atkinson, New Hampshire. We had good data on most of the children we'd selected except for Amy, who was one of the best writers. One day Amy was writing about cheetahs and composed an unforgettable line for a nine-year-old, "A cheetah would make a sports car look like a turtle." We had her texts, but we didn't have any information on her process. The lines emerged on paper as if they were being printed by a computer. We'd say, "Tell me about writing this, Amy." Amy just shrugged. "I don't know," she'd say in her squeaky little voice.

Well into our study she finally said to Lucy Calkins, a colleague and fellow researcher, "I think I know how I write."

Lucy quietly responded, "Tell me all about it."

"The other night I was sitting on my bed wondering how I would start my fox piece the next day. I said to my cat, Sidney, who was on the bed next to me, 'How are we going to start the fox piece?' But I couldn't come up with anything. About ten p.m. my sister, who is a junior in high school, came home and turned on the hall light. Now, over the doorknob where there's a place for a turn lock there's just an empty hole. When my sister turned on the light, a beam of light came through the hole and struck Sidney full in the face and Sidney went squint. Then I knew how I'd start my fox piece the next day."

In fact, Amy did write her fox piece and this is how I remember it: "There was a fox who lived in a den and over the den was a stump. There was a crack in the stump and a beam of light came through the crack at midday and it struck the fox full in the face and the fox went squint."

Think through how you make it possible for children
to rehearse their topics before they write them.

Requiem

David Munslow was a tall, stumbly kid in my fifth-grade class. He wore scruffy clothes and didn't say much. But David could draw. My friend Roy pointed to a sheaf of papers David was carrying (David drew on newsprint, shelf paper, any paper he could get hold of). "Show him some of these, David. Show him the ones of Lil' Abner."

I couldn't believe what I was seeing, near-perfect copies of Lil' Abner and Daisy Mae. "Draw one of Daisy Mae right now," I commanded. David quietly took his pencil and presented me with my own copy of Daisy Mae. Just like that. Right from his head.

We told our teacher, Miss Adams, about David. She said, "I'll have the art teacher, Miss Davis, take a look." Miss Davis came in and looked over his drawings. "Do you have any more? If you do, bring them in."

David did, and Miss Davis said, "I'd like you to go to art classes on Saturday at the Rhode Island School of Design. I'll speak to your mother about it." She did, but the lessons cost money, and David's family was poor, and there was no way for him to get a ride.

Roy and I believed in David and wanted him to be famous. We tried to earn money to help, collected quarters and dimes, but it just wasn't enough.

One Saturday in May David was playing down by the millpond. He must have stumbled on some rocks and fallen into deep water. David couldn't swim, and he drowned. We were all so sad. I was angry. I thought, *If he'd been at art school on Saturday he'd still be alive.*

> *The death of a classmate is especially*
> *hard and very confusing to children.*

Losing It

David was a grasshopper. That's what the other teachers called him. He just couldn't sit still. (*Attention deficit disorder* hadn't yet entered our vocabulary.) David was also active in making trouble in the classroom. He was clever in his way, and very quick. Students complained, *David poked me, hit me, took my pencil*. Noise usually emanated from wherever David was. I rarely caught David in the midst of causing trouble. But one day I saw David ready to jam a pencil into the side of another boy. "David!" I shouted.

"I wasn't doin' nothin', Mr. Graves," his reflex response. But this time I had him dead to rights. Seething with anger, I walked to where he was standing, reached over, grabbed his shirt collar, and literally lifted this small sixth grader off the floor. His bulging eyes brought me to my senses. The class was deathly silent.

That was Friday. I spent the weekend alternating between feelings of remorse and fear. (Today I could be sued and tried in court or barred from the profession for life.) However, David had a strict and demanding father and may have seen worse at home.

I was waiting for David on Monday morning. I called him aside and said how sorry I was for what happened on Friday.

David looked bewildered. "What happened?"

"When I reached over and lifted you up. That was dead wrong."

"Oh, that's okay, Mr. Graves. "You had to."

"No, I didn't, David. And it won't happen again." We had a different relationship after that. But I didn't tell anyone else what had happened.

Teachers, like doctors, need to be able to share traumatic
events in their teaching lives anonymously.

So Much Advice

I once had a terrible flu from which it took me months to recover. People would see me dragging about and ask how I was. "Not very well," I'd reply. My wife and friends, meaning well, bristled with comments and advice:

"I took this miracle stuff and was back on my feet in days."

"Have you been to the doctor yet?"

"Maybe you should try another doctor, get a second opinion."

"Your trouble is you work too hard; this was bound to happen."

"Are you sure this is just flu, not something else?"

"I once had the same thing; took me months to pull out of it."

We've all been there. The suggestions spin inside our head, and we get mired in self-doubt.

Shift your perspective to children who struggle with school. From the time they get on the bus until they return in the afternoon they also get comments, advice, and questions, from a host of people:

"Sit still on the bus. Don't walk in the aisles when the bus is in motion."

"Where are your books? You didn't do your homework. You should have an assignment book."

"Must you wear the same clothes every day?"

"You made a good start here."

"If you keep on with this kind of work, I will have to give you a failing grade."

"I like the way you are continuing to read this book."

"Do you think your parents know how poorly you are doing?"

"We're sending you for evaluation. Nothing seems to be working."

How is a child to make sense of all this information, some of it conflicting, year after year? The more problems a child has, the more often adults enter his life with advice and recommendations.

Let's help at-risk children make sense of the enormous range of comments and advice they receive from so many adults.

Ask the Children

I was the director of reading and reading clinics for a small city in western New York in the mid-sixties. There were five reading clinics throughout the city, staffed by solid reading people. I worked hard to develop their skills.

We had workshops on using informal reading inventories, perceptual assessments, IQ testing, auditory and visual assessments. I was studying for my doctorate at the time, and I wanted to make sure that we covered all the informational bases for analyzing children's reading problems. Later in my career I realized that we never asked the children what *they* thought their reading problem might be. Simple statements like *tell me what happens when you read* or *tell me or show me how you read that* are a good opening. Maybe the child feels she has no problem at all. If we sense the child feels there is a problem, we can say *show me here where it is hard for you* or *why do you think reading is hard for you?* The child first has to gauge whether we really want to know what he thinks; otherwise he may just say whatever will maintain the status quo.

It is very important to get the child's perception of events, especially in the teaching of reading. The child may have an erroneous perception we need to deal with. The child may be thinking, *And when is she going to get to my problem in reading?*

> *When a child is confused about something, first ask,*
> *with real curiosity, "What do you think is going on here?*
> *I'm sure you've thought about it. What's the best way out?"*

The Specialist

Brian stood on the auditorium stage answering questions about whales. He had just reenacted a nineteenth-century whale chase. He'd built a model of a whale ship and constructed whales out of papier-mâché. He'd taken the audience through the process: darting the sperm whale, the Nantucket sleigh ride, the sounding, killing the whale, and finally hoisting it to the masthead and cutting the blankets of blubber off the carcass. The children sitting on the floor of the gym auditorium were breathless.

"Are there any questions?" asked Brian.

"Did a whale ever sink a ship?"

Brian paced back and forth giving due academic pause. "Yes, the cutter Essex was sunk by a large sperm whale off the coast of Chile in 1822. The whale was actually named Mobius Dick, made famous by Herman Melville in his book *Moby-Dick*. Mobius Dick was finally done in by three cutters off the coast of Japan some three years later." Next question.

It was an important moment for the audience because Brian showed them what it meant to know a subject with some authority. It was even more important for Brian. He'd hardly been a reader the previous October. Now, in May, he was demonstrating what "specialty reporting" was all about. During this project every child in the school had became an "expert" on some area of interest: they read books and articles, kept notes, wrote a piece to show their knowledge of the subject, interviewed someone who knew more than they did, and finally gave an oral presentation. Brian had gone from being a diffident student to an assertive learner.

Children can develop a sense of what it means to know
by pursuing special interests over several months.

Level the Playing Field

I wasn't prepared for Christmas the first year I taught. Children kept giving me sly glances as the day approached. I heard, "Don't look, Mr. Graves!" more than once.

We had a small Christmas party the day before vacation. I served cake and ice cream, the children exchanged cards, but I hadn't expected the gifts that appeared out of their desks. I unwrapped the packages reluctantly, under their beaming scrutiny. I received eight bottles of aftershave, two sticks of deodorant, two neckties, etc. I was lifted by the wonderful spirit in the room.

Then Andy sidled over and said quietly, "I would'a got something for you, Mr. Graves, but my mother wouldn't let me." I went from the highest high to the lowest low. I said warmly, "Andy, that's okay. I'm so glad you are here." But I could tell my words weren't enough. He genuinely wanted to do something but couldn't. I knew then that next year I'd set up different ground rules. Everyone ought to be able to give something of themselves, but there would be no bought presents.

The next year I ended a long class discussion about the holiday by telling them they could make or write something for the person whose name they drew, but they couldn't spend more than fifty cents.

Only noncommercial gifts should be permitted at school parties.

A Safe Haven

Some schoolchildren are downcast on Fridays, especially before a full week's holiday. They know what a long stay at home means. They know they won't be safe.

I sat next to a seven-year-old girl on a flight from Baltimore to Manchester, New Hampshire, last week. (Southwest Airlines has open seating, and I had an eye out for a child sitting alone.) "I have to visit with my father one weekend each month, and my stepmom will meet me at the airport when I get there," Jessica said. She didn't have any sad tales, thank goodness, but we did have a lively conversation about books, her teddy, and one of my books. I wondered, though, about the disruption in this child's life and that of the many other children whose living arrangements are determined by court order.

We've all heard about children who are assigned to weekends with mothers who have abusive boyfriends. The mother doesn't protect the child or may have a drinking problem herself and loses touch with what is happening. Or a boy is physically abused by a father who is angry because he is out of work and wants to make someone else hurt because he does.

Other children have to stay indoors because the neighborhood isn't safe. To go outside their apartment means being open to predation by older children or adults in the building or on the street. Their parents often work two jobs, and these children sit alone for three or four hours at a stretch.

School can be a safe haven where children like these encounter caring teachers and friends with whom they can work, chat, and enjoy real companionship, a place where they can grow up safely.

*Look over your class today. Are there some
children who fear being at home?*

"You Like the Writing, But I Like the Drawing"

Six weeks into gathering data for my dissertation in a second grade, I was pulled up short when one of the children, Michael, said, "You like the writing, but I like the drawing." I'd been continually asking him questions about his writing while ignoring his drawing. He'd usually start by making elaborate drawings in the space above the lines where he composed his writing. I'd show up about the time he completed his drawing and started to write.

The next time he picked up a large eighteen-by-twelve-inch piece of paper and went to work, I made detailed notations. He spoke as he drew: "This guy is going to fall into the water and a whale is going to eat him." Then he drew the man falling and the whale with jaws open wide.

I realized that Michael was using his drawing to rehearse what he was going to write later on. But when I compared what he said in his drawing with what he said in his writing, there was much more information in the drawing.

When children make value statements, we need to pay attention.
Listen to words of value in your student's language
and ponder what is behind these statements.

The Sound in the Head

I was in Toronto conducting a writing workshop with a group of teachers. One them, Mr. Green, a published writer of adolescent fiction, told me a story about one of his students that had a great effect on me:

"I'm used to reading aloud to my class. I guess I'm pretty good at it, because my students obviously enjoy it. I usually put in a few flourishes of interpretation from my vantage point as a writer of fiction. One day one of my struggling students, a tough kid, came up to ask a question.

"'Mr. Green,' he said, 'You know when you read aloud and it sounds so good? Like when you sit and read that stuff to yourself, does it sound like that too?'

"I thought for a moment and said, 'Well, it isn't exactly like reading aloud, but I sort of hear the reading, what's happening on the page.'

"The boy replied, 'Mr. Green, I don't hear nothin' like that at all. It's all quiet.'"

Some students see what is happening. Others both hear and see. But sadly, for many there isn't much happening at all.

How well do we know what is happening in our student's heads as they try to take in a text?

Chewing

One day I sat chewing on a pencil, trying to write, and a poem came to me. I thought, "I've been chewing for a long time, ever since first grade." I laughed as I wrote. Often details come quickly when I'm remembering something funny. Laughter is such a reliever of tension.

In First Grade

In first grade
Everything is edible; soft,
Primary pencil wood
To run my teeth down
Like corn on the cob.

Second course is paste
During reading while
Miss Jones' yellow eye
And green smile catch
Me in midmastication
Of a primary chairback
During story time,
Fresh erasers nipped off
The end of a borrowed pencil
Or brown art gum erasers
Offered as hors d'oeuvres
From the art supply cabinet;

Then I reach for the fragrant
Golden ends of Delores Gallo's hair
Hanging over the back
Of her chair and on the books
On my desk.

At recess rawhide webbings
In a baseball mitt, then green
Crabgrass pulled just so
To gnaw white succulent stems
Like salad at Sardi's.

Who needs warm milk
And graham crackers smelling
Of the janitor's basement
At the Webster School
When we're already seven courses
   in?

The details of children's behavior are
fascinating and often lead to poetry.

They Notice

One day in my second year of teaching I drove into the school parking lot with a used-but-new-to-me Dodge sedan. I was quite proud of having left my dented Plymouth behind and traded (ever so slightly) up.

Five minutes into my day three boys approached me. "See you got another car," said one.

"A Dodge Fifty," said the next boy. "Automatic transmission."

Their responses implied a lack of enthusiasm.

"Best you could do?" asked the third with a touch of respectful sadness.

I didn't realize it then, but now I do. Everything teachers do is under scrutiny. Wear new earrings, skirt, jacket, get a haircut. Place a stack of new books on your desk. Children are alert to what we do, wear, buy, and value.

If children are so observant about the details of our lives,
then we need to show them what we value when
we demonstrate how we write and read.

"We Hope You Get the Job"

Mary Ellen Giacobbe was demonstrating a writing lesson for a large group of Toronto teachers. The teachers watched as Mary Ellen helped fifteen young first graders choose topics to write about. The demonstration went very well. The children were enthusiastic as they discussed what they knew. They immediately started writing and shared much of what they had done at the end of the lesson.

As the children filed out of the room past Mary Ellen, who stood in the doorway, one of the children looked up at her with a smile of anticipation and said, "We hope you get the job."

Children's perceptions, especially those that reflect
their knowledge of the adult world, can delight us.

Living Within the Child

I'm used to doing workshops in which I work with children before a teacher audience. Unfortunately, the teachers focus on what I am doing, hoping to pick up a tip that will help them teach writing. That may stand them in good stead in the short run, but one tip is insignificant.

When I observe teachers teach, I focus on the children. The real story of what is happening lies within the children's understanding of the lesson, one another, and the relationship of the lesson to their own learning.

Once I orchestrated a special teaching demonstration. I worked with ten children, to each of whom I assigned three teacher observers. I asked these teachers to see the entire class through the eyes and ears of their child, to write down everything the child said, record nonverbal interpretations, note anything said to another child, anything I might say to the child. The point of the data was to try to answer these questions: "What does your child know? What does he or she want to know?"

At the end of the lesson each three-person team compared notes and did their best to answer the questions. When the child left the demonstration she left her paper on the desk or table at their location. Once the team finished their analysis they could pick up the child's paper and look more specifically at what their child knew by way of information, skill, stories, and knowledge hinted at. They also came up with questions they wanted to ask me or the child.

The teachers became very possessive: "Our child's hand was up and you never called on him." "You interrupted her and wouldn't let her speak." "You only called on the children who pushed for your attention." More important, they learned what to look for relative to a child's potential and where they might teach more specifically. In the end, they were much more aware of my teaching and how it affected their child.

Choose a student in your or a colleague's classroom and
spend twenty minutes observing how that child takes
and makes meaning from what's happening.

Achieving Focus

Helen Murphy, the remarkable Boston University professor, could give dazzling teaching demonstrations within minutes of entering a classroom filled with children she'd never seen. Her observations were precise, her decisions sound. Hers was diagnostic teaching at its best.

All of her colleagues were in awe of her skill. We aspired to her greatness in the same way that young athletes envision themselves becoming a Michael Jordan in basketball, a Barry Bonds in baseball, or the Williams sisters in tennis. We were duly impressed with Helen as a role model, but we hardly knew where to begin to acquire such skill. Helen brought thirty-five years of preparation to her teaching. She put on a good show, but what were the basic points, the fundamentals?

When I did demonstration teaching in my own school, I tried to copy Helen. I worked in high gear, showing enthusiasm and getting responses that were impressive—for one day. But I made so many invisible decisions that my teachers couldn't see. Worse, I allowed little discussion afterward. And I didn't do a follow-up lesson that built on the day before.

Several years ago my wife asked me to explain basketball. There was so much happening that I asked her to watch just one player and forget everything else that was going on. Focusing on one player helped her see the entire panorama of basketball. She saw the little things, how the player positioned himself for a rebound or ran for position without the ball. Demonstration lessons are important, but we need to help teachers focus within a room in which many things are happening simultaneously.

When teachers visit your classroom, don't put on a show.
Think about how to help them learn the most they
can about the children and your teaching.

PART FIVE

Supporting Reading and Writing

We've just come back from winter vacation and are beginning the second half of the year. Perhaps we want to reflect about life and literacy, specifically about the teaching of reading and writing. (Naturally, reading and writing breathe through all the daily reflections in this book.)

Above all, we need to think about our own reading and writing. And I'd add to these basics the reading of the world around us: stories from our own lives as we grew up, stories from the lives we lead now, stories in today's news. In every unfolding story, the teller wants to command our attention and then make sure we get the main point of what is happening.

Writing in an Oral Age

Ours is an oral culture, in a world becoming smaller by the second. This is the digital age. We live under a cloud of communication satellites that allow us to call our next-door neighbor, a colleague in California, or a friend in France—instantly, from wherever we happen to be. I am sitting in an airport. The man on my left is talking intimately with his girlfriend in San Francisco, the woman on my right is trying to close a deal with a client in Detroit. They speak into their cell phones loudly and publicly. We can now participate in all sorts of situations orally, right here, right now. And choosing not to do so essentially excludes us. We can be accepted, or we can be rejected. And we crave acceptance; we want to attend the party.

Young children participate in this global network of conversations as well, using cell phones their parents provide. The parents call to see how things are, the children phone in updates on their whereabouts. Children also call each other. They need never be apart from their friends.

I applaud any time someone gives voice to their feelings, sets up contacts with others, or explores new thoughts. I think back to my great-great-grandfather on a whaling ship in the Pacific, who had to wait six months to a year for his wife's letter answering his letter. But his letters survive today, and I can participate in his joy and sorrow. I understand his dreams and feelings as if he sat in the next room. I want to embrace him.

We need writing more than ever. Writing slows down the quickness of thought into a series of words that establish ideas. Writing is where we learn to think. Words come quickly to those who write daily, because the pathway to ideas and personal thought has been well established. I take a stab at a draft. When I come back to it the words are waiting; I can penetrate my thinking of yesterday and explore new ideas today. In time I stand behind these words and challenge the world to respond.

Look over your classroom week. How often are children creating texts that involve real thinking?

Reading the World

I'm the guilty party who said children should choose their own topics. Teacher complaints about the topics children were choosing—bad television shows, violence, insipid characters with little dimension—were lost on me, drowned out by the rain of my ideas on the tin roof of my ego. I simply said, "Start from where they are, then move on from there."

It finally dawned on me that what was missing was a demonstration of where good topics come from. Children need to see how people choose topics from their everyday world. I borrowed a term from Paolo Freire— "reading the world"—although I use it in a somewhat different sense. This is how it works.

First, I read my world and make a quick list. Here's yesterday's: *I'm sick, looking out the window; I'm waiting for the medicine to work; I'm learning new things on my new computer; I'm talking to lots of people to ask for help with the computer; I saw a moose.* On another day the world I read might include traveling on a bus, eating in the cafeteria, or walking down the hall. I keep changing locations.

If I'm with young children, I then create possible topics that are close to their interests. Once I have my list and have spoken a bit about each one, I ask them to choose the one they'd like me to write about. Often they have to vote. If the group is older, I talk aloud about which genre I might write in: personal narrative, fiction, an essay (because I have very strong feelings about an issue), or poetry (because there's a certain rhythm to the topic).

I want children to see that topics are right under their nose. I speak aloud about how wonderful it is to experience life over again through words. One of the great questions that any writer asks, at any age, is, *Why would anyone want to write?* In showing children the origin of topics, I'm also showing them why people write in the first place.

Observe the immediate world of the school bus, cafeteria, playground, to see how you might show children where writing can originate.

Have a Pen Ready

Nancie Atwell's eighth graders were quite excited about going on a Friday ski trip. Since her school is in a coastal fishing community, many of the students were inexperienced skiers. But that didn't diminish their enthusiasm.

The following Monday Nancie asked some of the boys how they enjoyed the trip. "We never skied," one responded.

"What do you mean, you didn't ski?"

"We got our tickets ripped off. We had never used a T-bar before. So when the bar came along, we tried to hop on instead of letting the bar lift us up. Anyway, we ended up laughing and falling in the snow. Of course, that pissed the lift operator off. He cursed us out and ripped the tickets off our jackets."

"That's terrible. So what are you going to do about it?"

"We can't do anything. He got our tickets, and that was last Friday."

"As long as you have a pen, it is never over. I think you should write to the owner and tell him what happened."

The boys poured out their thoughts in a first draft. Nancie looked at it and said, "Well, the owner will certainly be impressed with all this foul, four-letter language. How successful do you think this letter will be?"

The boys went back to work, opening with the line, "Your lift operator, Emil, does not use language appropriate for thirteen-year-olds." The letter went on to explain the facts of their case. They got a letter from the owner in reply thanking them for telling him their story. He knew the operator was a problem but no one had ever said it in writing. Any time the boys wanted to come back, they could have free lift tickets.

No unfortunate or unjust situation is ever over as
long as we have a pen with which to respond.

Where's the Heartbeat?

I came up with a new question about a month ago: *Where's the heartbeat?* It means, *I'd like to see some motion, flow, involvement, strong interest, caring, in this piece of writing.* Not everything we do makes our heart beat a little faster. Often, we just get to work and in the midst of putting in our time discover something new. Until then, there is no heartbeat.

Experienced writers or artists, who know what it is to put in hours on the mundane, have that sense of anticipation, the feeling something is just around the bend. They feel in their bones that something will come up out of the muck. Their heart does indeed beat a little faster, and they keep working until it is suddenly *there,* staring them dead in the face.

For many students there is no heartbeat in anything they do in school. There is no anticipation, because anticipation is based on past discovery. They've known only failure and punishment. To put a foot forward, to put down a few words, is an enormous risk for them. But there are also students who *can* write, read, do mathematics, who outwardly at least just don't care. Their hearts may beat to music, friends, or events far afield from school.

I've read many student papers that have no heartbeat. There's no one there. I shift into second gear. I read the student's nouns, looking for a story, a question, some why behind the words.

The heartbeat leads us to the voice, or the voice leads us to the heartbeat. I'm always looking and listening for the heartbeat: a chance remark, a line, a noun, a shout about something the kid cares about, a song the student is humming.

We need to look for, listen for, and feel the heartbeats in our students. That's where the energy is, for us and for them.

The Why Behind Human Behavior

I was in West Des Moines, Iowa, sitting in the teacher's room, when Lola Mapes confronted me about the fiction her students were writing. "I'm so sick of it," she said, "violence, horrible things; what do you recommend?"

I said, "May I use your class to demonstrate a possible solution?"*

"Be my guest," she said. As we strode down the hall, she shouted into the office, "I want a video camera in my room in five minutes!" I began to understand Lola's power in that school.

The children had just come in from recess. I called them over to the corner to sit on the floor with me. "We're going to create a story together, but I want you to choose the topic." There were three suggestions: someone kidnapped, a boy on an island all alone, and a father and mother arguing about a divorce. The divorce storyline elicited the greatest show of hands.

After we had chosen the family name, Dunderlin, I began establishing the characters. "Tell me about father."

"He says he's always tired. He sits there and stares at the wall."

"What is his occupation?"

"He's a doctor, and he says he's on call, but really he's got a girlfriend in the next town." I figured I'd better switch to a description of the mother.

"She's easygoing. She listens to the kids."

There was a big discussion about whether she worked outside the home or not. We finally agreed that she was a psychologist with office hours from nine to two. Just as we were winding up this portion of our work, a little red-haired girl, dressed very neatly, darted a hand in front of my face.

"And she's always cleaning." I challenged this characteristic, because the group had already said the mother was easygoing. "That's right, she is, but right now she's so angry she can't stop cleaning." The group agreed this was plausible.

When you treat yourself to creating fiction with your students, be sure they investigate the reasons for human action.

For a complete discussion of this workshop, see my book Experiment with Fiction (1987), pp. 28–32.

To Tell the Truth

Donald Murray, Pulitzer prize–winning journalist and professor emeritus at the University of New Hampshire, has been asked to demonstrate how he writes to a hundred or so English teachers. An hour is set aside for the workshop.

The English teachers get to pick the topic, and for the first twenty minutes the group is in wild discussion about what it should be. Someone finally says, "Murray isn't going to have any time to write if we don't decide and decide quickly." They settle on *write about your favorite place in New Hampshire* and call Don into the room.

"What's the topic?"

"Write about your favorite place in New Hampshire."

"Oh, hmm." (Murray said to me later, "I already had misgivings, but I tried.") He thought a moment, went to the chalkboard, and tried a lead. But he crossed it out and thought some more. ("The sweat was pouring down my back like you wouldn't believe.") He raised the chalk to the board a second time but knew before he started that it wasn't going to work. He finally turned to the group and said, "I can't write on this topic."

"Why not?"

"I have no favorite place in New Hampshire." He explained that to write well about this he really needed to have a favorite place. "Maybe if I thought for a long time, over several days, I might come up with a place, but probably not."

A writer can't suddenly write falsely. Writing with a voice that speaks the truth is what professional writing is all about.

How many prompts for writing assessments require kids not to tell the truth and therefore write poorly?

Less Is More

Student writers are usually rewarded for length. Rarely are they rewarded for brevity.

I once visited an inner-city school, an invited guest in an English class of high school freshmen. The teacher announced that Dr. Graves would be happy to be of assistance as they wrote their character sketches.

About fifteen minutes into the class a hand went up; I went over to assist.

"And how can I help you?" I asked the young male student.

"I've only written one line, and I'm stuck," he replied.

I looked down and read the line he had written. It captured the essence of his character in ten words: "When Ms. Bell yells, everyone's ass tightens just a little bit."

I said, "Now that's good writing. You've told us exactly what Ms. Bell is like. I'd stop right there."

We need to emphasize the power of brevity. Brevity requires much more thinking than lengthy passages do.

The Case of the Disappearing Essay

A veteran teacher told me this story about her principal.

"Our principal led a writing workshop in which he stressed topic choice, writing, publishing, the whole bit. He especially stressed topic choice. Late on the following Friday, I was working in my room when I looked out my door and saw him taking down one of the children's pieces from the hallway bulletin board. I challenged him: 'What are you doing?'

"He seemed quite startled (I guess he didn't know I was in the room), and said, 'Oh, this, well this piece is one big complaint about food in the cafeteria. Do you know how much trouble I'm having down there? If the cooks see this piece, there'll be trouble, big time.'

" 'But you told the kids they could choose their own topics. If you're going to take it down, you have to explain it to them.'

" 'Fair enough,' he said. He looked like he was glad he had the weekend to think it over.

"On Monday he summoned the two boys who had written the piece. 'When you interviewed the cooks about the food what did they say?'

" 'Oh, we didn't do that. They wouldn't like it.'

" 'Boys, I took your paper down because I don't think your work is done. You go down and interview them, get some more facts, see what they think, and then come back.'

" 'We don't know what questions to ask them.'

"The principal gave them a hand with the questions and off they went— and back they came with wide eyes. 'Do you know about government subsidies and surplus? Do you know what they have for a budget?' They went back to writing but with a very different point of view."

There are many different points of view. Help children
investigate and state opposing positions.

Valentine's Day

Of all the days on the school calendar, February 14 stands out as the one having the most to do, figuratively at least, with children's rapidly beating little hearts. For once, if only in a sappy valentine, kids have a chance to put "I love you" in writing.

Teachers often underestimate the power of love in elementary school, and the consequences of bringing love out into the open. When I taught, I'd catch children glancing dreamy-eyed at each other from across the room. Boys would corner me as I left the room, "Know who I love, Mr. Graves?"

As I think back to Valentine's Day at the Eldridge School, in East Greenwich, Rhode Island, I remember waiting anxiously for *the* card, from Elisabeth. No matter that I had ten other cards from girls. No matter that Elisabeth's card looked exactly like theirs and contained just her signature, no handwritten note. The thought of not getting a card from Elisabeth was anathema. I sighed deeply when I finally held the card with her unmistakable handwriting on the envelope. That was enough for me.

Of course, some children don't get *the* card, get only a few cards, can't afford to give cards. Some even get angry because a child on the social fringes *sends* them a card. Love is complicated in elementary school. (Which should come as no surprise: the joy and complexities of love never end.)

We need to be aware of both the joy and
complexities of love in our classrooms.

"Focus on the Writer"

Sometimes the simple lines that great teachers utter cut through to the quick of what we must do.

I was observing Mary Ellen Giacobbe conduct a workshop. It came time for questions. "Mrs. Giacobbe, I have this child who just keeps drawing, but he won't write. I also have some children who won't write *or* draw. What's your advice?"

"Focus on the writer and the writing will come. That means that you focus on every aspect of the child's life, what he can do that is good, what he is interested in. If you focus on the fact that he isn't writing or continues to draw, he will never get beyond that. There is always something in a drawing to respond to. And you know lots more about a child than that he isn't writing. In time these reluctant writers will turn around and produce. Just don't be in a hurry. Attend to what the child is doing."

Focus on the writer and the writing will come.

When Writing Succeeds

When education's focus on the writing process was at its peak, someone asked me, "When will you know that you've achieved your goal?"

I replied, somewhat facetiously, "When the public starts complaining about the content in the students' writing."

People's complaints about education are always along these lines: *Kids can't spell like they used to. They don't know grammar any more. Did you ever see such terrible handwriting? Listen to them speak; it's a foreign tongue, it isn't English.* So each generation of elders wails about the new generation of students, year after year after year. Just once I'd like to hear someone complain about content. I'd like to hear someone refer to a challenging essay or a satire about the town or village elders.

Sometimes student content does turn heads within the school. I know of four boys who decided to produce an underground newspaper satirizing the principal and various teachers. The paper was well done, and if the principal had had a better sense of humor he might have laughed with the boys instead of suspending them.

Show students how to write good satire or challenging essays that mean something to them, and their writing will improve: they'll have reasons for using conventional spelling and grammar.

Learning Conventions

Frank Smith said that every act in writing is an act of convention. It strikes me that we teach conventions backward. That is, we teach conventions from the standpoint of not making mistakes: *you forgot to capitalize, you need a period here, where is the serial comma?* In fact, children should know which conventions they already use accurately, which ones they are trying to learn, which ones they'd like to learn in the future.

Why not begin with conventions they already know and have students make a list of them? Work with five children at a time and talk over which conventions they can put on their list. Begin simply. "How many of you put spaces between words? How many of you compose from left to right? Why are these conventions important?" (Remember, it's a great day for kindergarten or first-grade teachers when their writers first grasp these very simple precepts.) The point is to help children add more and more conventions to their list.

Children also need to try out new conventions. Conduct minilessons on conventions all the time, so that children can experiment with them in their own texts. For example, show the serial comma and ask if anyone is already using it. Immediately move into how the serial comma helps the reader. This is the important thing: how the convention helps the reader understand what the writer is trying to communicate.

Conventions also help the writer: if the writer ponders how to mark off the text so that she as first reader will understand it, a better text results.

Children need to learn conventions in the
context of why they are important.

What the Public Prizes

Harold Rosen once said to me, "Any idiot can tell a genius how to spell a word." I laughed, because I have experienced more grief from parents over misspelled words than any other aspect of the curriculum, when research shows there is no correlation between the ability to spell and intelligence.

In the nineteenth century, being able to spell and having "a good hand" (good handwriting) were considered more important than a diploma. In a recent survey of American parents asking which elements in the curriculum they thought were most important, spelling ranked right behind reading and mathematics and was rated more important than the ability to compose a worthwhile text. (How interesting that text is prized less than the spelling used in it!)

Obviously, schools are and will continue to be judged on how well the students spell. The opinion that good spelling and handwriting indicate a sound education is still very much with us. And it is true that writers must be considerate of their readers. It is a mark of etiquette to be thoughtful of the person who will attempt to read what we have written.

Spelling is prized more than writing—the thing it serves—when writing is essential to the future of our world and culture.

Authoritative Language

Wyslawa Zymborska, a Nobel laureate in poetry, taught me a new way of listening to institutional language. She had lived through the German and Russian occupations of Poland and in her Nobel acceptance address shared her views of authoritative language.

She began with humor. "They say the first sentence in a talk is the most difficult. There, that's out of the way." She then went on to say very important things. "I can always tell a dying institution by its use of language. It is the language of authority and control, has little life, and it loves to use absolutes like always, never, and must." She went on to show that it is the range, aptness, and flexibility of language that demonstrates the ability of a culture to respond to challenges from without.

I now can't help but notice that politicians by and large issue edicts. They seek not to persuade but rather offer absolute statements, usually with no supporting details. How often do leaders present both sides of an issue and then state their own view, giving the impression that much thought has gone into what they are telling us? That should be the natural language of a democracy, and it is rare these days.

We need to help children with their use of absolutes. They begin with absolutes by virtue of being children. They need to learn to take in other points of view and shift their language accordingly if they are to be persuasive.

The language of persuasion is essential to the health of a democracy.
How often do your students write or speak persuasively?

Sharing Writing

When children share writing from the "author's chair," it is very easy for them to lose control of their subject. A child tells about losing a tooth, and suddenly everyone has a lost-tooth story. A child shares a story about his trip to the doctor and sits forgotten while the other children roll up their pant legs to show scars from accidents or operations. Or perhaps his peers raise so many questions that the child wonders where his writing should go next, if anywhere.

There is a way to help both the class and the child who is sharing. First, the class needs to earn the right to make comments and ask questions by restating for the author—who must listen carefully—the details included in piece. When the class finishes this phase, I turn to the author and ask, "Are there any details that we missed?" Then, if the class is older or more advanced, I may ask, "What is the one thing this piece is about, it's focus?"

Second, the class may then tell what struck them about the piece, what feelings were engendered by it. These may be similar, opposite, more tangential. Afterward, I may turn to the author and ask, "How do you feel about what the audience has said?"

Finally, the class may ask a few questions to help the writer flesh in more details.

This procedure helps both the writer and the class listen to each other and produces much better texts.

Children need to earn the right to ask questions or make
suggestions by first showing they are good listeners.

Who Writes the Problems?

A number of years ago I was asked to talk about writing to a gathering of the American Society of Engineers. As I recall, they were mostly professors of engineering. I had no idea why they wished to have me come. I am no mathematician and even less an engineer. Nevertheless, I accepted—too quickly, with too little forethought.

As the date drew ever nearer, my tension rose. There had to be some reason I was invited. I pondered what I could say. I couldn't even think of an opening line. I'd have to take a wild stab at something, guess at what I could contribute to their discipline. I decided to open with a question and pray that what I had to say about writing would reach them.

I stood before my audience on the appointed day and asked my question as clearly as I could. "I'd like to see a show of hands: at which point do your students have the most difficulty, when they read the engineering problem or when they do the math related to the problem?" The 80 percent–20 percent split indicated that students could do the math but didn't know how to read the engineering problem.

I then asked, "How many of your students write engineering problems?" One or at most two hands. "Writing is the making of reading. I would be willing to bet that if your students wrote engineering problems, they would be able to read them better."

Have your children write problems across the
curriculum. Begin with one simple area.

Teaching Like Tolstoy

Few people know that Leo Tolstoy, the famous Russian novelist and author of *War and Peace,* started a school for peasant children on his estate at Yasnaya Polyana in 1861. The peasants had been given the right to vote, and he saw literacy and learning as essential to becoming a good citizen.

First traveling throughout Europe to investigate current approaches to teaching, Tolstoy was appalled by what he saw. Children were being taught systematically, being told the attributes of various objects, memorizing isolated facts, but never being asked to apply that knowledge. It was frozen in the category it was first learned.

Brimming with enthusiasm, Tolstoy was determined to teach his peasant children differently. He let them explore the sciences and continually questioned them about what they were learning. He also had them do a lot of writing. The children were filled with the master's enthusiasm.

One day when he made his usual announcement, "It is time to write now. Take out your tablets," the children replied (he encouraged an informal style, remember), "We're sick of writing. It is your turn." Tolstoy thought for a moment, then said, "Yes, I suppose it is my turn. What should I write about?"

One child said, "Write about a boy who steals." They then gathered around Tolstoy's desk to watch him write. "'The boy, Fedka, looked around the room.'"

"Stop," they cried, "No boy named Fedka would ever steal." Well, thought Tolstoy, I suppose that is the wrong name to choose. The children observed and listened as the writing unfolded. Tolstoy would stop and ask their advice. He was astounded at their knowledge and observations, both about telling stories and about life. Later, Tolstoy published his article "Are We to Teach the Peasant Children to Write, or Are They to Teach Us."

It is always good to show children how writing
unfolds and the types of decisions that go into it.

No School Today!

Whenever I spot an oncoming storm on the weather map, my heart lifts at the prospect of a no-school day. In New England we have, generally, snow-storms or hurricanes. I suspect that tornadoes, floods, and ice storms have a similar effect in other parts of the country. Or maybe a flu scare or an outbreak of lice sends the children and teachers home for the day.

At any rate, I follow the weather closely, every day. A storm in Florida always piques my interest. East coast storms start in Florida and make their way up the coast. At Cape Hatteras, in North Carolina, they often bend east and go out to sea. But if they continue north and reach New York, our hearts beat just a little more quickly.

Who is that creature within me, the one who craves a day off from teaching? Teaching is such an intense activity that perhaps I long for the gift of relief. If school is canceled, I'll linger over coffee, actually read the paper, play with the children, read the book I've been waiting to complete. I've been up since dawn watching the local cancellations crawl across the bottom of the TV screen. Will I go back to bed once I know? Probably not. I'm too filled with adrenalin, the adrenalin of an unexpected reprieve.

What things relieve the intensity of teaching
for you? Think of two or three.

Be the One Teacher

When I was conducting my study for the Ford Foundation back in the mid-seventies, all the people surveyed were asked: "Tell about a teacher who saw something good in your writing and then helped you to say it better."

Seventy percent of the people couldn't remember anyone who had helped them, 23 percent mentioned one teacher, another 7 percent mentioned two such good teachers. No one remembered more than two good teachers of writing, yet those one or two teachers had made all the difference in the individual's ability to write today.

Everyone can't be a good teacher of writing. But if one building has at least four good teachers of writing, it will change the quality of writing in the entire building.

*Be that one good teacher of writing who sees the good
things children are capable of and therefore shows
children how to express what they know and feel.*

94

Book Talk

Last week I conducted my current workshop, for about two hundred teachers, on energy in the classroom. I decided to interject a new ingredient. "Make a list of three books you've read in the last year, then tell your partner about them." The room erupted with the energy of good book talk.

*****

"I'm into books on horseback riding. I'm a rider myself, and I compete at shows. There's some good stories in here about famous riders who have won some of the best cups."

*****

"Don't you love books by Barbara Kingsolver? Her characters are real. I don't know how she picks them up, but they have so much dimension to them; I can even say 'I had a friend like that once.' "

*****

"I'm reading a book about Russians in Maine. As a kid I used to summer in Richmond, Maine, where there was a settlement of displaced persons from Russia. They'd always hoped they could go back to Russia, but now they are very clannish and stay only to themselves."

"I wonder if maybe Mainers sort of let them stay that way. We're sometimes a little clannish too."

"Well, they wouldn't let us come in the house when we delivered some food at Christmas time. But the next day a lovely handpainted work of art showed up on our doorstep."

*****

I thought about how quickly they got to discussions about people in their own lives and how little they talked about *what was your favorite part? who were the main characters? tell me about the setting.* Those are school-type questions.

How often do you and your students genuinely talk together about the books you are reading?

A New World

It is January in western New York. The snow is deep and the wind is blowing. Two days ago Carlos Juan was in tropical Rio Piedras, in Puerto Rico, tending the pigs. Today he is wandering big-eyed in his new English-as-a-second-language classroom. Carlos is fourteen years old, and his large brown eyes are eager for discovery.

I watch him explore the room. He moves to the shelves and picks up small toys. He doesn't just look at them. He lifts a toy truck to his nose, rubs the sides, and turns it to different angles, perhaps simulating driving it. Next he picks up a stuffed animal and investigates it the same way. I don't believe he knows the English word for truck or the other items. Later we learn that Carlos Juan is not literate in Spanish. His journey will be a long one. Nevertheless, I am struck by his elemental and instinctive approach to new things.

Vygotsky says that when we encounter new things, we should increase our sensory engagement—that is, bring in sight, sound, touch, and smell—which is precisely what Carlos Juan was doing. I know that when I read an insurance statement, for example, I subvocalize, maybe even read it aloud, to increase my sensory involvement, or I talk it over with my wife.

Too many new language programs ignore the need for increased sensory experience, moving too quickly to fill-in exercises on sheets of paper.

Observe your students: do they increase their sensory experience when they encounter a difficult problem?

Language as a Sensory Experience

I can still sing the six or seven songs I learned in Spanish class fifty-five years ago. We learned the songs by ear, without text. Our instructor reasoned that the beauty of the words and their sound and rhythm would become part of us. When he thought we knew them well enough, then he gave us the texts and we translated them.

In the early days of ESL I had children from other cultures teach the songs and dances they knew to the other students. This created a community of respect. I remember the day two new children, one who spoke Arabic, the other, Serbo-Croatian, left class, each jabbering away in his own language, laughing and smiling, and using every means they could—hand signals, body posture—to communicate that they welcomed their new friendship.

I remember another day, one I spent in a second-grade classroom. What struck me when I read their writing was the range and precision of their verbs. Children often know nouns, but verbs are another matter. It is hard to get from one to place another without a good verb. I complimented the teacher on the children's writing and asked her how she did it. She enumerated the usual: she let them write every day, they chose their own topics, she and the other students responded to their writing. It wasn't until the end of the morning just before lunch that I got my real answer. The children had a period of movement exercises that they took turns leading. One would say, "Let's slither like a snake." All the children slithered. Next, "Tiptoe softly." "Rotate and spin." Ah. Bruner states that the enactive domain, the body memory system, is one of the strongest.

How wide is the gate for helping language be part
of a broader sensory system in your classroom?

Playing the Convention Game

The convention game is based on the premise that everything we do when we write is an act of convention. That is, words need spaces before and after them, punctuation separates and ends ideas, spelling helps us understand the words. These conventions exist for the reader and are a courtesy for them. But they also are there to help the writer know how to mark off meaning so even the writer knows what he means with greater precision. Here's how the game works.

First I group the students into teams of three players each. Children have their folders or portfolios on their desks. They may also have some of the books they are reading. I have a series of cards on which there are a wide range of conventions: quotation marks, semicolons, serial commas, various capitalizations, etc.

I hold up a large card depicting a convention. The teams immediately go to work to find this convention in their own writing. Failing that, they turn to some of the books they are reading. The first person in the team to find one quietly says, "I've used it, right here." The team then discusses what the convention is and why it is appropriate to use it where the child has, as well as how it enhances the meaning of the text. Once everyone understands, all three raise their hand.

Everyone in the team must understand, because I can call on any member of the team to explain what the convention is and how it enhances the text on the child's paper or in a book they are reading. I usually wait until at least three teams have their hands up before calling on someone in the first team to give an explanation. I give five points for a correct use of the convention on a child's paper and three points for identifying the convention in a book.

Experiment with the game. The key is for children to state how the convention contributes to meaning.

One Reader to Another

Back in the mid-eighties the members of our research team were trying to help the teachers in a particular school make the transition from basal readers to children's literature. We were all learning together, and it took six months of experimentation by both the teachers and us to finally arrive at a satisfying approach.

There were plenty of books to go around, and the children were soon reading one after the other. Then the teachers said, "That's fine, but how do we know they are understanding what they are reading?" We instituted journals in which the children wrote about their books and the teachers responded with questions: *Who was your favorite character? What will happen next?* The children responded as briefly as possible, slipping into a gear reminiscent of filling blanks in workbooks.

One of our team members said, "When people talk about books, they don't use language like this. They go back and forth talking about content but in a much more appreciative or critical way."

One of the teachers said, "Maybe if we write about the book first and then ask for comments, we could go back and forth with decent dialogue." It worked, but teachers were overwhelmed with how much time it took to respond to each child.

Our ultimate solution was for children to exchange book talk with a partner and for the teacher to write to each child once a week. At last almost all of the children and teachers were engaged in serious book talk and writing.

Authentic book talk involves an interchange between two readers, both of whom are curious about what the other is reading and why.

PART SIX

Getting Personal

I*t's almost spring, time for a change of pace. As I look back through more of my life, I invite you to look back through more of yours. The book about our life comprises many volumes from which we continue to learn. All of us have traveled some rocky roads, learned some tough lessons about knowing, living, and loving.*

Let's have some fun thinking about our own reading and writing. Who were our mentors? Or maybe we've learned to ski or have mastered the art of gourmet cooking. Everything holds the germ of a story that invites reflection; even our cookbooks brim with our history.

Who Do You Think You Are?

Viktor Frankl's incarceration in a Nazi concentration camp was an endless round of belittlement and humiliation. But one day it dawned on him that no Nazi could assign his personal worth. Rather, it was up to him to say to himself that he was an intelligent human being, created as someone who was able and willing to give love and service to others. From that day on he refused to accept the Nazis' version of his worth. They could make him do things, but they could not control the value he attributed to himself.

Our profession is besieged by critics at every turn—politicians, administrators, parents, all harp on the lack of standards in public education. They cite data comparing our children with other children. Rarely, very rarely, have any of these critics watched us teach. Until they cross the threshold of our classroom doors we will not listen to them.

We do need feedback on our professional practice, but that feedback must be wisely selected, must be specific, and must never undermine our worth as human beings. We have great value and are willing to be great learners.

We are in charge of our value as professionals and have a right to demand respectful, specific feedback on our classroom performance.

Smarter, Not Harder

I don't often fly first class, but this flight was a long one, coast to coast, and I needed to stretch out and work. The man next to me was deep into the graphs and charts on his computer screen. When he came up for air, we greeted each other. He was the CEO of a growing software business. With a touch of pride he confided, "We're about to go public this very next week." Since I was in the middle of my study of human energy, I asked whether I could interview him. "Sure," he said.

I asked, "On a scale of one to ten, how do you rate your energy level?"

"Say, that's a pretty good question. Hmm. I guess I'd give myself about an eight."

The number people assign themselves is unimportant. Their interpretation of the number is the significant part of their answer. "What makes it an eight?"

"Well, I'm on the road about three weeks out of four. I have everything I need right here," he patted the case at his feet, "I can be reached anywhere at any time, and I expect the leaders in my company to be prepared in the same way. Our company is on the move. I put in fourteen-hour days, call my ten-year-old son on the phone every evening. He's a whiz at computers, you know."

"Okay," I said, "What would it take to go from an eight to a ten on the scale?"

"Very interesting," he said. "Never thought of that. Let's see. There's this guy I know who is CEO of another company in my same area. He gets so much done, but it doesn't seem to take great effort. I can't really tell if he is high energy or just plain smart. Hmm, what would it take? I guess the real story is efficiency, not energy level. Or maybe it's both. Saving energy by expending energy more efficiently." In other words, work smarter, not harder.

Wise teachers are always looking for ways to save energy by observing their students and their use of materials, resources, and each other.

But for Whom

Who are the five most influential people in my life? How do I know? So many people have taught me things. Maybe this series of questions will help me decide: *Who's been present over many years? Who caused a shift in my life's direction? Who taught me a particular skill that has had lifelong implications? Who's stood by me at a time of crisis? Who was my most important teacher?*

Many years. For my first eighteen years and many more after that my mother was my chief interpreter, teacher, questioner, and above all pusher. I was a dreamy kid who continually needed a good shove. Mother's most frequent directive to me was, "It's time you. . . ." Dad was influential too, but not as much as Mother.

Shift in life direction. Rev. Dr. Gary Demarest suggested I stop being a principal and become a minister of religious education. Although we were only together for three years, his influence as a preacher and teacher is highly significant. I continually draw on what I learned from him.

Particular skill. Donald Murray taught me to write. Even though my dissertation was filled with educational jargon, Murray showed confidence in what I knew, then guided me toward clear language that reflected a newfound voice.

Stood by and with me. Betty, my wife of nearly fifty years, stood with me as I finished my dissertation, walked with me through any number of personal and professional crises, raised our children and grandchildren, is the first reader of all my writing, and is my partner in interpreting the world.

Most influential teacher. Professor Donald Durrell, an aggressive educator, produced a paradigm shift in how I viewed children, prepared materials, and demonstrated for teachers. I think I have kept the best of what he taught. I have drawn on his influence for nearly forty-five years.

For better or worse who have been the
most influential people in your life?

We Are What We Read

Which five books have most influenced my personal and professional life? Again, so difficult. Here are the questions I'll ask to limit my choice: *What book has influenced me throughout my life? What book caused a turning point in my life? What book do I refer to again and again? Does a certain genre influence my life more than others? What book has affected my thought most recently?*

Question 1 is easy: the Bible, of course. Though there have been lapses off and on, I have engaged in serious, systematic study of it as well as taught both the Old and the New Testament. The more I dig into scripture, the more I see the human story unfold, especially in the Old Testament. Jesus' teaching in the New Testament is essential.

Turning point? I suspect that Jerome Bruner's *The Process of Education* was a turning point. When Bruner stopped me cold in the early to mid-sixties, I continued to see teaching, learning, and knowledge itself as continually unfolding, not static.

I refer again and again to Lewis Thomas' collection of short essays about the biological sphere, *The Medusa and the Snail*. There is much wisdom in these essays, and I often read them aloud and cite them in my work.

Genre is a tough one. It's is a toss-up between poetry and biography, and biography wins because I read four or five of them a year. But can I cite one particular biography? When I was in Scotland working on *Writing: Teachers and Children at Work,* I read Irving Stone's biography of Charles Darwin. Darwin's dogged pursuit of the species revealed a very meticulous, humane, struggling scholar. I've reread the book two times at least.

My most recent influential book is Margaret Wheatley's *Leadership and the New Science.* The scientific basis for systems theory and human ecology that she reveals has heavily influenced my view of teaching and learning.

What's your list of five most important books?

Two Readers

I'm fascinated by readers—their reading habits and which books they enjoy. What do books do for him? for her? for me?

My wife Betty reads more than I do, at least two or three books a week plus magazines, newspapers, and whatever I happen to be writing. Betty has a number of "reading stations" throughout the house—books and papers in disarray on a table or patch of floor—and she's always ready to talk about what she's read. She's also a member of a book club. She reads more nonfiction than fiction simply because she always wants to learn something new. And she usually takes something to bed to read, sharing elaborate details I can't understand as she turns the pages. Since Betty is a night person and my day begins at five a.m., I often must resort to a gentle, "Don't you think it's time to turn out the light?" But over the years I've received the equivalent of at least one master's degree and another doctorate from listening to her talk about the things she's read.

I'm a different reader. I read sections of books with intensity but read a book from cover to cover perhaps only once a month. I might read two books of fiction a year. I read most of my books on vacations, when I have larger chunks of time. I read widely and vocationally. As a boy I pondered fictional and nonfictional characters and wondered what I might become when I grew up, and I'm still pondering those questions and decisions. My books are carefully arranged in categories so I can find them when I need them. I read widely in history, psychology, and more recently, science and technology. Reading has always been a means to a personal, philosophical, pragmatic end. The short list of authors I continually reread and quote includes Lewis Thomas, David McCullough, Farley Mowat, Eamon Grennan, Raymond Carver, Billy Collins, John McPhee, John Jerome, Annie Proulx, Margaret Wheatley, and Bailey White. Poetry is a special love, and I have a huge section of books by poets and about poetry in my library. And of course there's a section of books about education.

What are the last three books you've read?
Who do you talk with about them?

The Crucible

Traumatic events can have a profound effect on our lives. Some people call them make-or-break situations. Warren Bennis and Robert Thomas, in their book *Geeks and Geezers* (2002), call these events *crucibles*.

I had one such moment in college. My major professor gave me a D+ for my major paper during first semester of my senior year. A friend of mine had been killed in Korea a few weeks earlier, and the paper was on the pacifism in Leo Tolstoy's *War and Peace*. My professor wrote but one line of comment, "Please change your typewriter ribbon."

I went haywire, failed three midterm examinations, and was put on academic probation. I felt humiliated as a learner and as a human being. Admittedly, the paper was not a good one and was filled with errors of punctuation and grammar. On the other hand, the professor was unable to see beyond my errors to my genuine emotional struggle. I managed to graduate, but the scars of his response have lasted a lifetime.

I compensated by going on study binges during my time in the military: anatomy, the Russian language, psychology, Russian history and government. I had to prove to myself, if no one else, that I could learn. I saw no chance of attending graduate school; my grades would show I was not worthy. And even though my postmilitary jobs as a teacher and principal went well, this litany still sounded in my head: "You've fooled the people around you, but some day you'll be found out."

I finally sidled in the back door of doctoral study as a probational student. I remember my first class, in which I virtually memorized the assignments and, indeed, whole sections of text. I was afraid I didn't belong. I leaped into discussions, asked questions relentlessly. Everyone wondered, "Who the hell is this guy?" I studied so hard and worked so incessantly because I needed to show that I *did* belong. Eventually, I received my doctorate, and my dissertation won an award from the National Council of Teachers of English.

What have you learned from the crucibles in your life?

Finding My Voice

People often comment that speaking before groups seems to come easily to me. I do feel comfortable with most audiences now, but that has not always been the case.

When I was seventeen I entered a speaking contest. Halfway through my mind went blank, and the trauma of that moment stayed with me for the next ten years. I developed a kind of phobia for speaking in any kind of group, even one involving only informal conversation.

Finally my voice became hoarse from all the tension in my vocal chords, and a specialist put me on total voice rest for three months. I learned many interesting things about myself and others during those three months, but none of them had to do with solving my terror at giving a formal talk or in entering into easy conversation.

When I entered the service and was stationed in Boston at the U. S. Coast Guard base, the terrible hoarseness in my voice still with me, the military doctor sent me to Massachusetts General Hospital. The doctors tried to help me speak in a different way, one that would release the tension from my vocal chords. What they didn't realize was that the tension was psychological, the fear that I might not be able to complete a sentence or I'd say something wrong or I'd embarrass myself.

The turning point occurred shortly after Betty and I were married. I needed to speak about stewardship in our church, and I felt so strongly that people needed to give of themselves that I lost all fear and spoke from the heart. Suddenly I had a different voice.

Our voice often takes hold when we have a conviction
about a matter of great importance and speak up
in the service of something greater than ourselves.

Friends Who Can Disagree

Rob, my psychiatrist friend, is interested in everything from Mac computers, quantum physics, cycling, and Eastern religions to cosmology. Everyone needs a good friend who is sincerely interested in learning yet isn't afraid to ask demanding questions.

One day, as we walked up a road, Rob asked, "Are you enjoying the sound of authority in your voice?" I could listen back several lines and indeed my tone was, "I'm the authority on this matter." Facts speak for themselves or they don't. I didn't need to add the authoritative tone.

I do the same with Rob. He frequently arranges his thinking in hierarchies from elemental predatory behaviors to considerate mentoring. The structures have been developed over many years with his clients. When I'm lost I say, "Rob, please give me an example of that. I know you can't share data about your patients but give me a 'for instance.'"

What we do share is a love of learning and that love allows us to challenge our ambiguities and displays of authority.

Learners are not afraid to disagree and give good
feedback for tone or the need for a solid example.

How I Began to Study Writing

I was one of four doctoral students at the State University of New York at Buffalo who drove the short distance to the home of Marion Cross, in St. Catherine's, Ontario, had a picnic together, and discussed our thoughts about dissertations.

As we went around our little circle, each stating his or her notions about research, I was relieved to be the last to respond. Most were seriously considering research in reading. The university had a very strong reading department. But I was made uneasy by its focus on what children couldn't do, what ailed them, or what was needed to correct their "deficiency." We bandied about such terms as *minimal cerebral dysfunction* and investigated problems with eyes and the fovea. I was also studying the work of Piaget and had taken a few courses in anthropology. When Piaget and Alfred Binet were studying children's intelligence, Piaget became fascinated with children's "wrong" answers. He thought they were merely giving answers to other questions. But what were these other questions?

By the time the group came to me, I was sure I didn't want to investigate reading. Suddenly I blurted out, "I think I will study writing." My friends asked me how I'd made my decision. I said, "I don't want it to be reading, and I want to explore new ground in writing. No one is doing writing."

That summer I did an independent study in which I reviewed the research on writing up to that point. Influenced by Piaget's studies, I realized that no one had sat down and observed children while in the midst of writing. What was their process? What kinds of decisions were the children making? I did pilot studies while seated next to children and discovered that what children did was not what textbooks said they did or needed to do. Children were smart little decision makers, and we needed to understand much more than we did.

Make a list of three things today that you wish you knew more about.

We Do Not Speak by Words Alone

When I was first in the ministry I was very fortunate to be on a staff where the senior minister, Rev. Dr. Gary Demarest, was an outstanding preacher. People often say, if you want to improve your tennis game play with someone who is much better than you are. The same could be said of golf. In this case, I had fifteen months to be near one of the best preachers in the country.

I wasn't privy to his process, so I had to guess at what was behind the product. He seldom used notes (except for quotations), never lost eye contact with the congregation, spoke with authority, and occasionally stepped from behind the pulpit to make major points. His sermons were carefully researched and very well organized; he was not only teaching and revealing a text but heading toward a destination, a final point, the congregation could anticipate. There were no surprise endings. Rather, we participated to such a degree in every aspect of his sermon that we all came to the satisfying and inevitable conclusion at the same time.

When Gary taught or spoke informally, he never let a table, lectern, or similar barrier come between himself and his audience. Our messages are not conveyed through words alone but by our full physical presence: facial expression, eye contact, posture, arm motions, even the distance between speaker and audience, all must complement the text.

> *How do you speak to your students, their parents, your colleagues? What are you saying with the hand gestures you use, the posture you assume, the distance you keep?*

Lead Time Is Seed Time

I spend roughly two months preparing for my talks, the same for my writing. When I have fixed the date and general topic for a talk, article, or book, I immediately set up a file (both an electronic and a physical version) and slot into it related articles, reflections, e-mails, Internet material.

The first month I also spend about ten minutes every day letting any and all ideas in—"If there's no surprise for the speaker or writer, then there can be none for the listener or reader." I enter them in my journal in answer to the question, "What is the one thing I want this talk or article to be about?" (When the product is a book, I add a little twist. I write the back cover copy of the book before I start writing any text. Back cover copy usually covers three things: *What is the book about? Who needs it? What are the basic contents?*)

Surprise usually lurks in the shadows and off the beaten path. Starting early allows me to go off on tangents. Many of the tangents don't get into the final product. On the other hand, they may be the beginning of the next article or talk.

Do you allow enough lead time when you need to speak at a meeting or function or are asked to submit something in writing?

Left-Handed Moves

I joined the U. S. Coast Guard, during the Korean War, with the hope that I wouldn't have to kill anyone. Nevertheless, in basic training, I learned to shoot an M1 rife with surprising accuracy. I didn't fully understand the technology behind modern weapons, but I could hit a bull's-eye at two hundred yards. I figured that if I killed someone who was two hundred yards away, I could fool myself into thinking I hadn't really done it.

However, one of our later classes was on hand-to-hand combat. We practiced a lot of judo moves: take-downs, body slams, hip rolls, disarming an assailant who attacked with a knife. The prospect of killing someone with my own hands with a chop or backward strangle was fascinating. I was a veteran of school playground warfare who more often than not came out on the losing end, and I felt a sense of power I hadn't known before. Day after day we practiced in the gym and barracks until we had achieved a new proficiency in defending ourselves.

Several months after basic training I went back to my college campus to visit with friends. They asked about my training, and I jumped at the chance to show my judo moves. I stood before a friend, poised, loose, ready, and said, "Make a move, any move." He made a move all right: he quickly shot out a left hand. I couldn't respond. All of my partners in training had been right-handed.

As teachers, we try to anticipate the actions of our children and students. Invariably, someone makes a "left-handed move," and we don't know what to do. But if we are wise, we learn from these left-handed moves and build up a repertoire of effective responses.

When was the last time you were totally surprised by
something a child did and weren't quite sure what to do?

I'm Easy

After writing sixty or so pieces for this book, I decided to switch from twelve years of writing in Word Perfect on a PC to writing in Microsoft Word on an iMac. To broaden the learning curve even more, I needed a different printer and added high-speed Internet access and a scanner. This was to be one magnificent, complete system.

First, a bit of history. My father was a terrible role model. He was a powerful worker, but he worked so quickly that he never stopped to see where he was going. I too act quickly, don't read the instructions, rarely ask others for help, and consequently end up at the point of no return, endlessly frustrated. My father also believed that all things electronic should be left alone. In the early days of television, when the TV screen was doing flips during John Cameron Swayze's evening news, I'd reach for the horizontal control. My father always stopped me midmotion: "Don't touch it, it will only get worse."

My friend Rob Richardson offered to help me set up the iMAC, since he was a long-time user of the system. He watched me try a few operations, noticing my self-doubt as well as self-recrimination. "Relax," he said, "slow down. Watch." Rob sat down at the keyboard, relaxed and comfortable, thinking the way MAC users think. Although it took him a fair amount of time to execute each step, he found it a joyful, engrossing game. Solutions were always just around the corner.

Realizing that installing all these separate pieces of equipment would take time, I followed Rob's lead and relaxed. I bought a headset so I could talk with technical support people and still work the keys. It was all just a matter of time, relaxed time. I encountered a side of myself that I'd never known. I laughed to Betty, "I didn't know I had a Zen side to me."

At last I have a new view of learning: relax, learn to forgive oneself for any errors, consult liberally, and one can't help but learn.

Try giving and getting intelligent feedback
in place of stepping up the pressure.

"What Could You Do If You Had Enough Guys?"

In May of my junior year of college something spontaneous occurred that I've never forgotten. Just after dinner on a warm spring evening my two roommates and I lazied our way back to the dormitory, lingering by the tennis courts to chat. One of us posed a simple question: "What could you do if you had enough guys?" My roommates were physics majors. One of them whipped out his slide rule and began calculating. "Yes!" he crowed. "If each person in the junior class had a hammer and chisel on a scaffold, we could dismantle the brick wall at the south end of the dormitory in about forty-five minutes." We rolled on the grass with laughter.

Our laughter attracted a crowd, with more and more students stopping to listen to our wild speculations about what you could do if you had enough guys. Within thirty minutes there were fifty or sixty students calling out their own wild answers and laughing hysterically. When the laughter finally died down, everyone went back to the dorms to study. Final exams were only a week away.

At midnight the bell signaling the beginning and end of classes suddenly started ringing. Spontaneously we poured from our rooms, half dressed, still dressing, one question still on our minds: "What could you do if you had enough guys?"

We raced across the campus. Ten men picked up a VW bug and placed it on the library steps. Milk cans were hauled up flagpoles. The president's front door was nailed shut. Huge empty boiler tanks were rolled across lawns and placed in strategic locations to disrupt campus traffic. There was certainly power in numbers that night, the power to disrupt. At two a.m. we retired to our rooms.

I've often pondered the events of that night, the surge of energy that brought with it the feeling of sudden power.

What could happen if enough teachers and educators came together and speculated about what we could do for our children?

Pulling Together

When I was in basic training, in the U. S. Coast Guard, each company had its own race boat crew. Every Friday the companies raced against each other over a mile and a half course. The boats we raced were no ordinary boats—they were Monomoy surfboats, built wide and heavy so that ten sailors could row against the waves in angry seas.

I was the stroke oarsman, which meant that I sat right in front of the coxswain, who steered the boat and, more important, called the cadence I had to maintain. The rest of the crew then kept up with me as I followed the "stroke, stroke, stroke" calls. We learned to be machines, bracing our feet against a stanchion across the bottom of the boat. We rowed with our whole bodies, legs connected to backs connected to arms connected to hands that held the oar.

You began a stroke with your body leaning completely forward, both hands on the handle of the oar, the blade completely behind you. At the coxswain's command of "stroke," you pulled the oar through the water until the blade was completely in front of you. Then you snapped your wrists downward so that the oar blade flattened parallel to the water (so it could cut through a big wave if it came) as you returned the oar and your body into position for the next stroke. With weeks and weeks of practice, our crew was able to maintain a very fast cadence.

If an oarsman lifted his oar from the water out of step with the others, he'd "crab," or lose his balance and fall over backward. This usually meant that each of the men behind him would fall over backward as well, like dominos; often their oar would come forward and strike the man in front in the back of the head.

There is a certain joy in becoming a nonthinking machine, listening only to the "stroke, stroke" command. There is a feeling of completeness and power when each person does his part.

> *Children and teachers can know the joy of pulling*
> *together when everyone knows her or his role and*
> *the part each must play to achieve success.*

Running

In 1953 I transferred to Bates College from St. Lawrence University. Bates was nearer to where we lived in New England. During orientation I decided on a whim to go out for the cross-country team. It was one of the best decisions I ever made. I didn't have natural speed, but I did have endurance and managed to finish back in the pack in most races. However, I didn't run in my senior year or for the next nine years.

Dissatisfied with being out of shape I started running once again in 1964. I drove up to the hills near our home in Hamburg, New York, because I wanted to run where no one could see me. There weren't many runners in those days. People wondered what I was fleeing from, and the occasional dog enjoyed a good, vicious chase. Now, with occasional time-outs for illness or injury, I'm into my fortieth year running, at age seventy-three.

I didn't compete again until I was sixty-eight, and I did well in half-marathons, placing first, second, or third in my age bracket.

Besides being excellent exercise, running is marvelous for meditation and reflection. Life can be intense and the discipline of running is a great relaxant. It is rare when I don't return refreshed and filled with endorphins.

I find that running at eleven a.m. after a few hours of writing is especially rewarding, because I continue to write in my head and come up with new ideas. Also, the premise for four of my last six books came to me while I was running. In the last two hundred yards of a five-miler, the main question behind *The Energy to Teach* dropped into my head. I said to my running partner, who wasn't a teacher, "Tell me, what gives you energy and what takes it away, or is a waste of time?" She answered eagerly and couldn't wait to ask her friends the same question.

Sometimes we need to do something totally different,
something physical, in order to slip our mind out of
gear and allow it to assume a new configuration.

Weight Watchers

In spite of running for forty years, I've had a continual problem with my weight; my body seems to think it desperately needs to replace all those calories I'm burning. I'd emerge from each winter very much out of shape, carrying an extra ten pounds. By late August I'd have shed the pounds, or most of them, but I'd still be overweight according to the health charts. I finally had to put my ego to one side and admit that I couldn't lose weight on my own.

I attended my first Weight Watchers meeting in September, 2002. I quickly learned the points system and, being a disciplined writer, I had no trouble being honest with myself about recording what I'd actually eaten. The best thing about Weight Watchers is that it taught me how to balance my nutrition in the context of my life: load up on vegetables and fruit, keep meat to reasonable portions, drink lots of water, exercise regularly, and attend meetings. Knowing I was going to have to step on a scale each week—being accountable—kept me on the path to weight loss. Over the next nine months I lost thirty pounds.

Accountability is important in education as well, even though learning is far more complicated to measure. Children need to keep records of their progress on matters that are important to them. When they keep track of their own reading and writing every day, their productivity, their ability to use conventions, the genres they are able to write in, they become aware of how well they are doing.

> *Real progress occurs when individuals keep their*
> *own records of something they truly care about.*

"I Need Your Help"

Back in the mid-eighties, during the early days of my experience (battle?) with computers, I subscribed to a service out of Massachusetts that guaranteed that anyone who had a problem with their computer would be back in business within twenty-four hours. They had technicians on the road all over New England, reachable by radio and telephone.

One day my computer crashed, and I called the service. As promised, the technician arrived late the same morning. "What have you got for a computer?"

"Northstar Advantage," I replied.

"Shit," he responded with a frown. He did some diddling and checking then asked to use my phone. "Won't cost you anything, it's an 800 number." He dialed. "Harry, who's good on Northstars? Charlie? Have Charlie give me a buzz at this number." A few minutes later the phone rang.

"Charlie? Eddie here. I think I've got an A-drive problem here but I haven't worked on Northstars before. What's the procedure? Read the manual? Frig that. Just tell me. It's right here on the table in front of me." In another twenty minutes Eddie finished installing a new A drive on my Northstar and I was back in business.

After Eddie left it struck me that he and his fellow technicians had to service all kinds of computers: they never knew what they'd run into. What impressed me about Eddie and most people who work with computers is that they are unashamed to admit they don't know something and they know whom to ask for help. We live in the twenty-first century; hardly a day goes by that we don't have to ask someone for help. We'd better know how, and we'd better know whom.

Children need to learn how to solve their own problems, but they also need to know who can help them when they are stuck.

When the Class Is Not Whole

When I first began teaching I used to joke with my colleagues that my good students were often absent and the ones who gave me difficulty were seldom ill. "Where are my number one draft picks?" I'd say. Or, "That Arthur is something else. He sets my teeth on edge with that voice of his and he seems always to be here. Next time I feel the flu coming on, or a bad cold, I think I'll go over and breathe on him. But that would mean we'd both be out at the same time, so, no, that isn't a good idea." We'd get downright jaunty with our black humor.

I've often thought back on those early days of teaching. We focused so much on individual learners, individual progress, but what about the entire group?

I once sat next to the Orthodox bishop of Bombay, India, on a plane flight. We got to discussing the difference between East and West. He asked me if I was familiar with the parable of the lost sheep. I nodded.

"You people in the West," he said, "focus on the one, the individual, that lost sheep all alone. And that is good. But I think we have what you have, but more. We say, 'How sad, the group is not whole, one of us is missing.'" I've never forgotten that story.

I wish I had paid more attention when a student was ill, missing from the group, and that I had honored and welcomed his or her return to the classroom.

If we have worked hard to build a strong classroom community, then when a child is ill, absent, or has moved away, we will acknowledge that we have lost something important.

18 Crisis

Two other professors and I shared a single secretary at the University of New Hampshire. Invariably, she'd be working on a job for one when the two others would descend on her with a job that just had to be done for class that day.

One morning I entered her office with a sheaf of papers in my hand that I needed duplicated for class at four. I knew I was supposed to give her twenty-four hours' notice. "Sue, I know I'm late with this, but I'm really desperate to have this for class today." She smiled and pointed to a new sign she'd bought at the local stationers: "A crisis in your life doesn't necessarily mean there's a crisis in mine."

"Oh," I said, "I see what you mean."

"I'll do it this once," she said, "but I'm giving fair warning this is the last time." She was right, of course; we'd been taking advantage of her superior work skills.

But crisis is a word to think about. Listen to the evening news and count the number of times *crisis* is used or at least an extreme urgency is implied. The word means "turning point," an opportunity for a new direction. It does not necessarily mean an immediate response or action is required.

Education is rife with congresspersons, board members, administrators, and teachers all invoking the *crisis* word in order to trigger immediate action of one sort or another. The word is also used to justify suspending individual rights or encroaching on individual space and time. It bestows the power to make someone else do our bidding.

In a genuine crisis—a turning point that might affect people's health and well-being—we need to pay attention. Otherwise, we need to pause, reflect, and ask plenty of questions.

The Bus Driver

Betty and I were staying in a hotel in Bondi Beach, Australia, and wanted to do some shopping in Bondi Junction, about ten miles away. We took a bus. Bus drivers in America and England generally don't seem too pleased to have passengers. Our first Australian driver was a revelation.

"Good morning, sir." I was halfway up the stairs into the bus, and I glanced up. A young man in cap and uniform was smiling at me.

"And good morning, madam, lovely jacket you're wearing today." This was addressed to Betty, who was behind me.

I fumbled for change. "How much, sir?" I found myself echoing his language and style.

"Only thirty, sir. No hurry." On my way to a seat, I looked at the other passengers. They weren't wearing the usual strained, get-the-shopping-out-of-the-way looks. I soon found out why.

More people boarded the bus, but the driver never changed his style. He had something different and unique for each one.

"Nice day to go to town."

"Lovely suit, sets you right up for a good day in town."

"Can I help you ma'am? Got much to carry, haven't you." He sprang into action and helped the woman up the stairs.

"Hi, laddie, grab the railing. My, what a strong pull. The last step is a big one."

I turned to the man next to me. "Do you know him?" By now the fifteen or so passengers already seated were straining to catch the bus driver's patter, thoroughly enjoying his brighten-the-day attitude. We smiled at each other, an instant community. As the bus rode along its route, we began to check the queues at the stops, looking for people wearing interesting clothing, children, senior citizens. What would he say to them?

How quickly one person can change the mood of a day
through what they observe and confirm in others.
Can we do the same each day for our students?

"Does Everyone Know Everyone?"

There used to be a standing joke about Jane Hansen at the University of New Hampshire. No matter where she was, what meeting she might be leading, what social gathering she was hosting, she'd invariably begin, "Does everyone know everyone?" One or two people always responded, "No, I don't, " and one by one people would have to give their names and perhaps say a little something about themselves.

Even though we enjoyed ribbing her about it, mimicking her words, we all knew Jane was right. The introductions might take time, but if a group needed to work together for even an hour, it was important to know everyone's name and something about the person. And since people were always volunteering different identifying information, we got to know new things about people we'd been working with for years.

Jane has a knack for creating groups that know one another better than just their names. She's a relaxed midwesterner from Minnesota, genuinely interested in other people. She was raised on a farm in an era and area where neighborliness was the natural way of getting along. It was important for people to know each other. If someone needed help, a quick telephone call brought immediate assistance.

Personal writing and sharing that writing are hallmarks of all of Jane's courses. Once again, people get to know one another. People trust one another in Jane's classes and therefore trust their literate voices. Oral and written conversations begun in one of her courses always continue by telephone or e-mail or over coffee. Her students want to know more about each other and are very comfortable asking each other for help. Her classes are springboards to much broader learning and involvement.

How well acquainted are your students with what other students are reading and writing? Do they know what you are reading and writing?

When There's Not Enough

I've gone walking with my friend Rob Richardson every Wednesday noon for the past six years. Rob is a psychiatrist, is much into Eastern thinking, and is fascinated by physics, medicine, you name it. There isn't anything we won't talk about. Rob usually has a new theory about how the mind works, I'm always thinking about teachers and children. Sometimes Rob's thoughts tumble out so quickly and are so theoretical that I have to say, "Please give me an example of that. Put it into a human context."

One day he said to me, "I want to try a new question on you. Here it is: 'What is there that there's not enough of in your life, right now, this very minute.'"

"Say, that's a good question. Hmm. There's not enough time."

"Enough time for what?"

"Not enough work time, writing time, not enough time for Betty and our family."

"So, what's first in the 'not enough'? You've mentioned work time, writing time, Betty and family time."

"Well, there's not enough quality time with Betty. She has to be first in the not enough. If something happened to her, I'd have to say I never had enough time with her. This question really pushes at your values doesn't it? Of course, the next question that immediately comes up is, What am I going to do about it? I guess it is something the two of us will have to talk over."

The what-is-there-that-there's-not-enough-of question quickly gets at the priorities both in our teaching and in our personal lives.

Two Heads Are Better Than One

In 1959 I was chosen by Dr. Donald Durrell, professor of education at Boston University, to be one of a group of people who demonstrated team learning in the public schools. I was honored to be asked, but I had little understanding of what the term *team learning* meant.

Dr. Durrell, a tall, outspoken, aggressive man, wasted no time in the first meeting I attended. He quickly put us into teams of three to brainstorm the answer to one question, "How will we be of the greatest service to the children and teachers in Gloucester, Massachusetts?" We'd be leaving in two weeks to demonstrate team learning in all subjects in every classroom in the elementary schools, using our own materials.

Rapid-fire discussions took place in every part of the room, one person in each group recording what was said. Since I was new, I listened very carefully to what the two other people in my team had to say. I still carry with me today the basic principles I learned then:

1. Two heads are better than one, but for most brainstorming, three heads are better than two. Two children will often just share their ignorance. With four, one will often pull out and not participate.
2. No child should have to sit in ignorance.
3. Children have different rates and levels of learning. For work in math or reading, children should be teamed with others of similar ability.
4. For sharing, however, groups should be heterogeneous, so that children of all abilities can enjoy their accomplishments together.
5. The school day should be balanced with all-class activities in music, physical education, drama, poetry readings, choral speaking, and the like.
6. Children need to learn to do independent study through specialty reporting.

How are you helping your students learn to work together in teams?

A Brash Man

Dr. Donald Durrell was not a humble man. On the other hand, he rarely failed to put his own abilities on the line. Learning by doing was his hallmark. When he demonstrated in a classroom, he included all the children. Difficult children were his specialty.

A principal who was taking a course with Durrell asked him to stop by his school and administer an informal reading inventory to a difficult child. Durrell breezed into the office, asked for the child, and was told he was in the library. He found the child on the floor in the corner. It was obvious the child wasn't ready to read. Durrell placed a table over the boy on the floor, sat at it with a little girl, opened a travel book, and told the little boy under the table, "Be sure to stay there and not move."

Durrell and the girl began to read the book, and soon the boy's head emerged from under the table. Durrell said, "I told you to stay under the table," and continued to read. The little boy's head came up again, and Durrell asked, "Oh, are you interested in this book?" The three of them read together for a while, and then Durrell said to the little girl, "You can go back to class now."

He completed the informal reading inventory with the boy, placed it on the principal's desk, and went home. Later, he told us in class, "If you can get a child to do one thing that you wish, after that it's easy. But all the while you have to know what you want to teach and how."

When is the last time you got a recalcitrant student
to do one thing for you and himself?

E. Hall Downs

Donald Durrell was teaching a course in language arts methods at Temple one summer right after the end of World War II. After class, a man came to him and said, "You're teaching this course all wrong. Children should never be allowed to make mistakes."

Durrell allowed that teaching doesn't work that way. He checked into the man's background and learned his name was E. Hall Downs, he'd just been mustered out of the army as a full colonel, he'd been appointed superintendent of schools in a Delaware town, and he had to take one course in language arts methods before taking the job.

Three years later Durrell happened to be in the State Department of Education in Delaware.

"We have a curious jump in scores in this one small blue-collar town on the Delaware river," a colleague told him.

"Any explanation?"

"Yes, they have this new superintendent, Mr. E. Hall Downs, who is evidently doing a remarkable job. He sent out a letter requiring all parents in town to attend a meeting before school opened. They must have wanted to see this character who thought he could order them around: the place was packed. But Downs was ready for them."

This is what happened. Downs asked children from a prosperous "upriver" community ten questions and recorded their answers. He then asked children in his town the same questions and recorded their answers as well. He played both recordings at the meeting and then challenged, "Do you want your kids to stay like this, or do you want them to improve, speak and read well, and go to college like those kids up river?" Of course, all the parents wanted their children to improve. "Okay, then you've got to read yourself, require reading of your kids, learn to speak well, and we're going to check on you." The parents loved the challenge and it worked.

Sometimes, however wild, plans can capture parents' imagination.

Inside Work

A professor friend of mine was a conscientious objector during the Vietnam War. An English major in college, he was assigned to teach English to students in the welding section of a city trade school.

The students at the trade school were not that enthusiastic about learning English, writing, reading, or anything else that smacked of book learning. They were strictly hands-on and consequently gave their new, inexperienced teacher a very hard time. In desperation the new teacher went to the tradesman who headed the welding section. "You've got to do something to help me; these guys are driving me nuts."

The welder had worked his way up in the union and, after spending twenty years on the job, spot welding twenty floors up in the open air during many a cold January, had finally landed the plush job of teaching in a trade school. He turned to the new teacher and said, "Shut up; you've got inside work. Get on with it."

Even though teaching can be very difficult, when the weather outside is frightful we can rejoice that we have "inside work"!

The Box

My report to the Ford Foundation was due in two weeks, and I'd written but four pages. I was drowning in jargon and felt the pressure of a deadline. In desperation I called my friend Don Murray. He said, "Come on down," looked over my pages, and agreed with me: "You're back to your dissertation ways." I could tell that he thought desperate measures were required.

Don got up, left the room, and returned with a cardboard box, a knife, and some masking tape. "I want to try something on you that I've never had the guts to try myself." He cut a slit in the top of the box with the knife, sealed all the corners with tape then said, "You know your subject; you've lived the information. Put away your notes, put a clean sheet of paper in your typewriter, and write. Don't change a thing. When you come to the bottom of the page, put the page in this box, take another sheet, and keep on writing. At the end of the day bring the box back here, and I'll give it a read."

I didn't for a moment believe this crazy system would work, but I was desperate. I went home, and as I began to set down what was needed nationally in the field of writing I was surprised to find my voice kick in. At the end of the day I'd written fifteen pages. I brought the box to Murray. He unsealed it, read the pages, then said, "Now, this sounds like you, and the material is good. Keep going."

By the end of the week I'd written a hundred and twenty-five pages of fairly decent stuff. Ultimately, with Don's help, I cut the manuscript to thirty-five pages. The report was titled, *Balance the Basics: Let Them Write,* and won the David H. Russell award for excellence in research in 1982.

Sometimes it is important to lower our standards,
stifle our internal editor, and write from the heart.

PART SEVEN

Thinking About Learning

Someone once said, "You can't get out of bed without a theory," meaning that based on long experience, you expect that when your legs hit the floor you'll be capable of standing upright.

We also enter the classroom with a wide range of theories in tow. We operate on the basis of theories that we know and can explain to others, but we also rely on theories that are unstated and implicit in what we do. In other words, our deep-seated theories about learning, teaching, curriculum, and assessment influence our actions even if we can't or don't acknowledge them consciously.

As we swing into the home stretch of the school year, let's think a little more about why we do things. I'll set down some of my stories and conversations in hopes you can use them to jump-start your own.

We Think What We Feel

"Just the facts, Ma'am," requested Sergeant Friday of the woman whose husband had disappeared. But if Friday had listened a little more carefully to the emotion behind the facts, he might have solved the case more quickly.

Emotion is the engine of the intellect. Our feelings govern the direction of as well as the energy for our thinking. Emotions fed by ego can distort the mind in its quest for clarity. Emotions can trick us into doing things only to garner outside approval.

On the other hand the emotion of wanting answers and results sustains thinking over long periods of time. My wish to take beautiful photos of my granddaughter and grandson leads me to learn how to use a digital camera. I know that new ideas lurk behind ordinary phenomena. Therefore, although I have only a vague notion about what I may discover, I write about rowing and racing surfboats when I was in the U. S. Coast Guard, knowing that if I explore this memory through words I will uncover something I haven't seen before and add to my understanding of the world. The emotion of wanting propels my intellect and skill in anticipation of the satisfaction I will ultimately experience.

We need to understand the full range of our emotions and how they influence our own learning and that of the children we teach.

Wonder

Lewis Thomas, a neurologist and the Pulitzer prize–winning author of *Lives of a Cell,* was continually astounded by the wonders of the world, in medicine, in biology generally, in the specific mystery of how warts appear and disappear. He also enjoyed studying the origins of words.

Thus it was no surprise to me to find Thomas focusing on the origin of the word *wonder.* He went back to the Indo-European roots of the word and learned that the original meaning was "to smile in the presence of."

I watch a three-year-old boy walking with his mother. Their short journey, a hundred feet to the car, takes a long time: every leaf, cricket, and pebble is wondrous. I suspect the mother isn't aware that she wears a smile, and I find myself smiling right along with her.

Something about any discovery cries out for us to share our joy at having made it. As my wife and I walk separately through a museum exhibit, I am startled by a painting—I beckon her over to share my discovery, and we smile at each other.

I smile when I discover third grader Amy's line, "A cheetah would make a sports car look like a turtle." Where did such an apt metaphor come from? If children read and explore their texts with no preconceived notion about what they need to say, they are primed for wonder. If they have time to explore a garden, care for an animal, or listen to stories and poetry, wonder will be part of their lives, and sharing it will make teachers and children smile together.

What is the wonder index in your classroom?

Saying Yes and Saying No

I once sought out a counselor because my life was simply too busy. I was saying yes to everything. My list of things to do was long. I feared telephone calls, because surely the person would be wondering whether I might do thus-and-so. And I'd add it to my list out of guilt, thinking that if I could do just a little more I'd feel better about myself.

I bellowed to the counselor, "How do I say no to all these obligations? I've got to get better at saying no; that's all there is to it."

She waited for the breeze of my agitation to die down and then said, "You're asking the wrong question. People don't lose weight because they've said no to food; they lose weight because they've said yes to the right food. People don't say no to infidelity; they say yes to a long-term relationship. People don't say no to busyness; they say yes to the important things, and then it's much easier to say no to the unimportant things."

I held up my hand. "I get the point. I've got to reevaluate what is most important to me first personally and then professionally. It all begins with my deep, personal values."

The counselor spent the next seven weeks helping me decide what I'd say yes to, beginning with my marriage and my family and then moving to my career. What were the things I wanted?

"Well, I want to write and help teachers and be in classrooms. That's where I get my energy."

"Okay, now you can decide what you'll say no to."

> *What are you and your students saying yes to in your curriculum? That will clarify what you can say no to.*

An Extension of the Human Voice

When I was a junior in high school my friend Bob Jessup and I dreamed of becoming radio announcers. Bob's next-door neighbor was Arturo Toscanini's manager. Because Toscanini was the conductor of the NBC Symphony Orchestra, Bob's neighbor arranged for us to tour and visit the studios.

The excitement of observing real announcers on the job was uppermost in our minds. We watched the announcers read their scripts at their microphones, letting the finished pages float to the floor. Seeing how sound effects were produced was fascinating. As the tour wound down, the agent asked, "Would you like to hear one of Maestro's rehearsals?" We agreed more out of politeness than interest: he had arranged our visit and we were grateful.

He brought us into the engineer's booth. "Maestro allows no visitors, so I am going to turn on the sound in here and lift the curtain one inch. You'll have to get on your knees and peek through the crack."

In strode Maestro, his authority apparent. The musicians snapped to attention. He rapped twice on the stand, lifted his arms, and the orchestra began to play. I had never heard such a full, lovely sound. But after only four bars, Maestro threw his baton to the floor and took off into the second violin section and stopped beside one trembling violinist. "Stand up and sing it," he demanded. "Sing the opening bars." The poor man did so with a wavering voice. I felt for him. "Mr. _____, you don't know how to sing it. Until you can sing it, you can't play it. Always remember, every instrument is an extension of the human voice."

Every pencil, pen, or computer keyboard—every instrument for forming letters—is an extension of the human voice. The person must be present in the work or the sound will be hesitant and hollow.

Celebrate Differences, Not Similarities

As I read more and more about human biology, especially systems theory, I realize that we've gotten research backward. The purpose of research ought to be to find out how we are different instead of how we are the same. Standardized tests want to know how we fit in the box, not what our contributions outside the box might be. It is much cheaper to study fit than nonfit.

Jean Piaget began his career as a genetic epistemologist by helping Alfred Binet study the intelligence of young children. Piaget became fascinated by the children's wrong answers, not the ones that had previously been deemed correct. Piaget's logic led him to say, "Ah, the child has come up with an answer to a different question."

There was a point as we were assessing the data from our study of children in Atkinson, New Hampshire, at which I was trying to make the data fit the children. In desperation I looked out of my window toward the home of my neighbor, an expert on trees. Jim could look at a tree, assess its canopy in relation to other trees, check its bark and branching pattern, and speak of how unique that tree was in relation to all the other trees. It takes an enormous amount of knowledge to see differences. It takes much less knowledge to see similarities.

When children are perceived as unique as well as similar, their notion of themselves as learners changes for the better.

It's All in the Timing

The Greeks have two words for time. One is *kronos,* which is sequential time, in which events follow events according to a plan: spelling comes at nine, followed by writing at nine-twenty, and so on. (One teacher described her principal's devotion to *kronos* this way: "He's always scratching me where I don't itch.") The other is *kairos,* which refers to the fullness of time, when a teacher sees that his students are ready for a suggestion or a question that will trigger new learning quite independent of his plan.

It takes a certain amount of experience with and knowledge about both children and pedagogy to recognize the *kairos* moments. Although teachers have their *kronos* plan, they are continually looking for the teachable moment. They assess a classroom and design minilessons to fit the needs of a group of students. In short, good teachers are pragmatists, observing process and results and saying, "This isn't working. It's time to redesign."

Kairos time perches at the pinnacle of systems theory. It is the teacher's assessment of local conditions, individual children's needs, and the direction her teaching needs to take that produces her professional sense of timing. The teacher must be the captain of her own ship, taking in and evaluating all the data in order to make the *kairos* decisions that lead to good learning.

Teachers need the authority to make the kairos decisions
in their classroom that lead to real teaching.

Boys and Girls Together

There isn't a whole lot of debate about the differences girls and boys display in the classroom (and elsewhere). Generally speaking, boys are active, territorially defensive, even aggressive; they can project feelings but aren't very good at examining them. Girls, on the other hand, are more sensitive to emotions, less actively aggressive, better at seeing other points of view. When boys write, especially fiction and personal narrative, their characters are active. Their themes encompass the broader community, national and world events. Girls' topics are more centered on home and school. Young boys rarely include characters of the opposite sex, child or adult, in their personal or fictional narratives. Girls do. Good teachers need to understand that this is both biological and cultural, but they don't have to accept it as the status quo.

Children of both genders need help understanding their flip side. Boys need to get in touch with their emotions. When a boy writes about catching a fish, we need to ask, "Well, how did that feel?" When the main character in his fiction is overly aggressive, we need to ask, "How does both this character and his victim feel when he does this?"

Girls need to be helped to understand their feelings and encouraged to stand behind them—in all genres, but especially the essay. They need to realize that having feelings strong enough to elicit responses in others is normal and acceptable.

Take a boy's and a girl's writing folder or portfolio and
examine the territory, his use of person, her use of person.
What does this tell you about gender differences?

What the East in Hawai'i Has to Teach Us

I've learned much from my good teacher friends in Hawai'i, much that has changed my views about the sense of community in the classroom. I bring my Western view to the islands and as East meets West I question my values. A bit of background.

Hawaiian values are rooted first in the concept of aloha. Aloha, in turn, embraces the notion of one large family or 'ohana. Aloha is the common greeting given by Hawaiians and the aloha is the joyful, open embracing of all others in a synergistic relationship of love.

A Hawaiian classroom community therefore is a noncompetitive one in which children help each other to be better than they were yesterday. The teacher shows through her daily actions of inclusion how children are to regard each other. "Keahi has created a beautiful scene for our delight. Tell us about your underwater scene, Keahi." She welcomes the art piece as a wonderful personal contribution the entire class can enjoy. From a process standpoint she wonders for the benefit of the class how such a piece came into being. Keahi's art piece is not in competition with all others.

This is not to say that excellence is neglected in Hawaiian classrooms. There is a fine attention to detail and demonstration of process by the teachers. Most of all, children learn to help each other to go beyond where they are at the moment.

As in any classroom in the world there is a range of ability in Hawaiian schools. The notion of "behind" or set apart as superior or deficient works against the spirit of aloha. Such labeling or setting apart breaks spirit of inclusion. Careful work within aloha means that every child must feel they have a contribution to make not just for themselves but for the community as a whole. Indeed, it is the offering that is essential to the spirit of aloha.

When children share their writing, projects, or reading ask, "And how does this contribute to our learning here? How are you feeling?

Working from the Inside

People often ask David McCullough, an outstanding historian, if he is working on a book. He replies, "No, I'm not working on a book, but I am working *in* a book." He means that he is thoroughly absorbed by his research, his notes, and above all his writing, all of which take him inside a subject.

I was once talking with a student who was writing about Joan of Arc. She told me about her struggle to write the paper. "I gathered all kinds of information about Joan, but it all seemed so dry. The day I decided to write a diary as if I were Joan was the day I passed from outside my study to the inside. Suddenly, I could feel Joan's voice inside my own; the writing took off."

Children can't concentrate, can't focus, because they can't feel the subject. They are on the outside, looking at a mammoth project to which they don't know the way in. Offering them achievable standards and an easy writing threshold is one of the best ways to cut the project down to manageable size.

When I want to get on the inside of a project, I write an e-mail or a letter to a friend telling him about it. I also tell him what I'm discovering. Discovering something new is not only energizing but also the surest way to end up on the inside. I am constantly asking, "So, what am I learning here as I both read and write?"

Another sure way for me to get to the inside of a subject is to write about it every day the moment I take on the assignment. I write about it to myself. Soon I am thinking about it when I am not actually sitting there writing, a sure sign I'm on my way inside it.

There are many ways for students to pass from outside a subject to inside it. Think of how you can help them. Have children share the experience when it happens to them.

Wanting It Bad Is Good

Neil Simon writes in *The Paris Review,* "In *Broadway Bound* I wanted to show the anatomy of writing comedy." In the play, two brothers are talking. One says that conflict and more conflict are the essential ingredients. But his brother disagrees; he says the key word is *wants.* "In every comedy, even drama, somebody has to want something and want it bad. When somebody tries to stop him—that's conflict."

I don't think any statement by an author has affected me more than this one. I took it and used it as the theme for an entire book, *Bring Life into Learning,* about teaching writing through characters.

When I read fiction I ask, "What does the main character want and want badly? Who or what is trying to stop him? Might he have something in his own nature that is keeping him from getting what he wants?" When my students are writing fiction, I immediately ask, "What does your main character want? Why does she want it? Have you shown us that?"

History is shaped by people who want something to happen. Their want gnaws deep in their gut, they attempt to steer people and events and so affect the course of the world and its culture. Feeling as strongly as they do, they are bound to be opposed by those who feel the opposite way just as strongly.

When I am blocked, it's often because my vision for the piece is different from what I want to happen on the page. If a student is blocked in a piece of writing, I turn the paper over and ask, "Tell me your wish, what you want for this piece. Take ten minutes to write about how you are blocked."

There is hardly any human event about which we can't ask,
"What does the main character want and want badly?"
Listen to the want behind what your students say.

What You Pay Attention to, You Reinforce

When I was doing graduate work at the State University of New York at Buffalo, a doctoral student conducted an elegant bit of research that was the envy of the other candidates. His was a simple premise, "What you pay attention to, you reinforce."

Recognizing that mouthing and chewing behavior in kindergartners is often associated with tension, he counted the frequency of these kinds of actions in his test classroom to get a frequency baseline before he began. Then he conducted his study.

In the first phase he told the teacher to attend to the behavior: "Take your fingers out of your mouth. Don't chew on the pencil. Stop sucking your thumb." In this phase the mouthing behavior increased markedly.

In the next phase the teacher was told to ignore the mouthing behavior completely. This time the incidence soared even higher. Children did anything they could to get the teacher's attention—they would stand in front of her chewing on a pencil, for example.

During the final phase the teacher was asked to attend positively to anything constructive the children were doing and tell them why. "I like the way you helped Samantha. That way, we were able to clean up much quicker." In this phase mouthing behaviors dropped below what it was at the outset of the study.

*Choose one small aspect of curriculum and go out of
your way to attend to good learning with regard to it.*

What's Jazz Got to Do with It?

Winton Marsalis is the preeminent trumpet player in the world today. He plays both jazz and classical trumpet and is often a guest teacher at the best conservatories and schools of music.

In a tutorial he first asks the jazz group to play something for him. He writes, "They'll play a song that is about four or five minutes long—but everybody will solo too long, so that song will become eight or nine minutes. So when they're finished playing, I pick out maybe the first or second person that soloed and ask, 'Okay, what did she play? Anybody in the band, tell me what she played when she soloed.'

"One hundred percent of the time no one knows. One hundred percent— not 99.9. Not once in ten years or fifteen years—however long I've been out there—has anyone ever been able to tell me what a person who soloed played in the beginning of their song."

Marsalis' point is that in jazz everyone has to be completely tuned in to what everyone else is doing. The final point he makes is, "This is the thing that is so difficult many times to convince our younger students of: that it is important for you to view yourself in the context of everyone else."

This is also what it means to live inside a community, inside a classroom. I often check to see if children are listening to one another: "What did she just say?" "What kind of feeling was in his statement?" I also try as best I can to reflect back to children what they are saying. This is what stitches a community together. I'm all smiles when a child spontaneously speaks about what someone else has said.

After a child has spoken or shared in your room today, see whether other children have listened and can repeat what was said.

Lessons from a Golf Pro

"Here's a bucket of balls; hit 'em." I had come for a golf lesson, and I thought at least I'd get an initial lecture on the finer points of the game. However, the pro's terse, direct language didn't encourage discussion. I took the bucket.

I hit some balls and looked over at the pro, who seemed more interested in the golfers on another fairway. I hit some more balls, which shanked and hooked from left to right. That seemed to perk up his interest. "Just keep your head down and your eye on the ball." The path of the ball seemed to straighten a little on my next attempt. I looked over again and saw that the pro was now talking with someone standing just behind him. Finally he walked up to me. "Watch. Get comfortable. This isn't baseball and forget the home runs." He took my club, rocked lightly, and easily drove the ball about two hundred and fifty yards. "Check your grip like this." By the time I'd emptied the bucket of balls, the pro had given me four very useful tips for straightening my drive.

On my drive home I thought about how the pro had helped me learn to drive a golf ball. Talking was useless until he saw me perform. It also struck me that with all his experience, he must have observed twenty things that were incorrect in my technique. Mentioning them all would only have confused and disheartened me. Instead, he chose the most basic; the rest could wait. In retrospect I also appreciated his directing some of his attention to other fairways and golfers. To have had him standing there watching my every move would have only made matters worse. He only needed a quick diagnostic glance.

*It's so easy to teach too much at once, overcorrect, or chose the
wrong next best thing to teach. We need to take our time.*

In Their Own Words

One year Ken Burns spoke at the University of New Hampshire's midyear graduation. Burns had recently completed his Civil War series for public television. In his films, he approaches history through the characters that create it, showing us still photographs of those characters while on the soundtrack well-known actors give life to their words. At the end of his address Burns read Major Sullivan Balou's letter to his wife back home in Maine. I have taken his letter and lined it into poetry without changing one single word.

Sarah, my love for you is deathless,
It seems to bind me with mighty cables
That nothing but Omnipotence can
    break,
And yet my love of country comes
    over me
Like a strong wind and bears me
    irresistibly
With all those chains to the battlefield.

The memory of all the blissful moments
I have enjoyed with you come crowding
Over me, and I feel most deeply grateful
To God and you that I have enjoyed
Them so long. And how hard it is for me
To give them up and burn to ashes
The hopes of future years when God
Willing we might still have lived
And loved together and seen our boys
Grown up to honorable manhood
Around us. . . . If I do not return,
My dear Sarah, never forget
How much I loved you, nor

That when my last breath escapes
Me on the battlefield it will whisper
Your name.

Forgive my many faults
And the many pains I have caused you,
How thoughtless, how foolish
I have sometimes been.
But, O Sarah, if the dead can come
Back to earth and flit unseen
Around those they love,
I shall always be with you
In the brightest day
And the darkest night
Always, always, and when the soft
Breeze fans your cheek,
It shall be my breath,
Or the cool air your throbbing
Temple, it shall be my spirit
Passing by. Sarah,
Do not mourn me dead. Think
I am gone and wait for me
For we shall meet again.

When you discuss history and the people who make it, ask your students how they feel about these events and people.

Artful Living

These are fast times. We are made restless by any kind of delay. Waiting for an elevator, we stare at the needle or electronic indicator showing the location of each one of a bank of elevators, our bodies poised to speed toward the first one available. If there is no indicator, we keep pressing the up button as if that will make one of the doors open more quickly. We want to get on with the next, the next, the next.

Last evening I was listening to ninety-two-year-old Ruth Gruber speak about her latest book, *Inside of Time: My Journey from Alaska to Palestine*. She was supposed to catch the weekly flight from Nome to Point Barrow, but every Tuesday there was some reason the pilot couldn't fly. Nome was a pretty desolate place and she dearly wanted to leave town. Finally, she decided to relax and get to know the natives of Nome, to "live inside of time" as she calls it, and that led her to new and delightful insights into a beautiful people.

"Living inside of time" leads to artful living. Georgia O'Keeffe explains her approach to teaching art this way: "When I teach my main point is not to teach them to paint pictures but to show them a way of seeing. When I teach art I teach it as the thing everyone has to use. There is art in the line of a jacket and in the shape of the collar as well as in the way one addresses a letter, combs one's hair, or puts a window in a house."

Both of these remarkable women show us how to live. Artful living helps us live inside of time, and that creates a sense of peace. We stop trying to force time to keep to our schedule. Rather, we focus on the people around us and discover both the beauty within them and in the world itself.

How can we teach so that our children live inside of time and
therefore connect with one another and their world,
discover learning instead of speeding through it?

The Quantum Leap

Bear with me today. The reading will be demanding. I'm going to try to explain as clearly as I can why local control is very important in public education and is especially important for teachers. Indeed, it has a very sound scientific basis.

Two famous physicists, Nils Bohr and Eric Heisenberg, were trying to explain what happened to atomic particles by using principles of Newtonian physics. But the old theories could not explain the wave and particles they observed. For three long years they struggled to understand until they realized that nothing could be generalized from one experiment to another. Under the old Newtonian physics a law could be transported and applied in a brand-new context. Indeed, context was unimportant. Bohr and Heisenberg now said, "Context is everything because the data you gather depends completely and solely on local circumstance." No experiment is replicable anywhere else. Thus, quantum theory and systems theory were born together.

This means that data derived from one child cannot be compared with data relative to any other child. Each child is unique; every teaching situation is completely different from any other; every school is a totally individual social unit.

We make comparisons between children at great peril
and certainly provide no help to teachers or children.

Jazz and Systems Theory Applied
to the Classroom

One of the best metaphors for understanding systems theory and quantum physics is jazz. Jazz, like systems theory, allows for individuals to listen to each others, yet play in harmony to make a beautiful sound. Each group has its own unique system and sound.

Like jazz, and reflective of systems theory, the best classrooms are based on self-discipline, an awareness of each other. And there are those wonderful moments when a class is aware that its cooperative behaviors are creating something new and special. I have seen classrooms come together when they seek to help someone in need. Perhaps someone in their room or another is ill and needs help. The class visits a nursing home together and learns to appreciate the elderly by bringing items to them that they've created themselves. Such projects require help from everyone. The focus is less on each other but on the goal all are seeking.

Quantum physics views all objects relationally. Everything affects everything else and the result can be harmony or dissonance. With people there is not perfect harmony. Sometimes there are days or specific times when a group of musicians will transcend themselves in an improvisational high and create great music. In one sense systems theory and good jazz are the ultimate in democratic expression. The same can happen in a classroom.

The success of America and our system of education has been its ability to improvise since its beginning as a republic.

Think back to events in your classroom when the children
created something new, something beyond them and they knew
it as a unique contribution. Ask the children to plan another.

PART EIGHT

Thinking About Assessment

Evaluation. *Just the word is enough to bring on a bad case of hives. But good assessment is important. As the renowned systems theory writer Margaret Wheatley points out, "What we need is good feedback, not bad measurement." Our students need to know how to evaluate themselves, and we need to show them ways they can do that.*

It's easy to get the numbers. Computers whir, scanning pages of blackened bubbles, then spit out the tallies. But we have to determine the qualitative markers that reveal the good thinker/learner.

If children have been reading books, writing regularly, and doing good thinking in mathematics—if they have developed their own voice and can defend what they think—they will do well on standardized assessments. It doesn't take them long to learn about tests and test formats. We can relax and continue our day-by-day reflections. The flowers of genuine accomplishment are blooming right alongside the weeds of normative rankings.

Defining Excellence

Most everyone seems convinced that testing will raise standards. A higher score means that good learning has taken place. In some cases that may be true. But I am concerned that the focus on numbers will convince us that we have fostered and measured excellence when we haven't.

Until excellence is spelled out independent of a number, I will forever be suspicious of test scores. For example, part of a definition of a good reader should be that she or he can compare books and critically relate one author to the other. Standardized assessments can't measure that very well—so do we leave out that ability just because it is difficult to assess?

Here's another definition of a good reader: "The student demonstrates an appetite for developing his own reading list in relation to subjects that interest him." Once again, assessments can't determine this, but what teacher wouldn't prize this ability in a child?

The problem with most definitions of excellence is that they require students to do or answer something someone else wants them to do or answer. And this is an important part of assessment. But we need students who demonstrate initiative, interest, drive, independent thinking, and the ability to think on their feet.

Standardized tests touch on only a narrow band of the rich, complex qualities that ought to be part of the good-student profile.

Your Personal Best

I enjoy running, and most of my race preparation involves putting in the miles at a steady pace. Some days, however, I do tougher work, push myself, and expend great energy. When race day comes, I relax and enjoy the race—I'm ready. It's enough to show up and participate.

Afterward, I enjoy chatting with other runners: "How did you do?" "Well, I established a personal best in the 10K." "What's your next goal?" "I'd like to lower my time. I need to do more speed work, and then I'll be able to overtake a few more people in my age bracket."

These are the kinds of conversations that ought to go on in schools. I want my students to have realistic goals that we have set together. Further, students should understand what it takes to improve and have some way of evaluating change. When children feel they are competing against everyone in the class, including the super learners, the notion of personal improvement is lost.

Work with one child today to help her learn about a personal best.

"This Is the Way We Do It"

I was visiting classrooms in Scotland as part of a study for the Ford Foundation. I wanted to see good writing, and I certainly did.

One boy, Ian, had written a particularly fine poem. I asked him how he had come to write it, expecting him to say something like, "I was standin' o'er the moor, the moon off to me right, the fog gently caressin' the low points, and I thought a poem."

Instead he said, "I'm from Aberdeen, and this is the way we do it."

What a lesson that was to me. There was a standard of excellence in place, an excellence connected to a responsibility to birthplace and heritage, that prompted effort and quality.

What are the elements in your classroom in which students take pride?

The Emperor's Clothes

Students in New Hampshire take standardized tests in April. It's a rite of spring observed by many other children across the country. I've never forgotten the following incident, which took place one such April.

A woman I knew was a marvelous teacher. She used a lot of children's literature in her teaching. The children in her room could discuss authors and their writing as well as any I'd ever seen. They knew good writing when they saw it and could usually sense when their own writing was good as well.

One day this teacher was about to administer a standardized reading comprehension test. Her voice hardened a little when she gave the instructions. She was very systematic. She wanted the children to realize that when she said, "Begin," they were to do their best. "Be quiet, say nothing to others, and answer the questions."

Minutes after the test was under way one of the children shot up his hand. The teacher pointed down to the child's desk with a menacing gesture—get back to work! The child did so but soon raised his hand again, this time waving it wildly and disturbing the children around him.

The teacher quickly stepped to his side. "What?" she whispered in her most severe tone.

"Who wrote this anyway?" questioned the child. "This writing doesn't have any voice."

"I know," said the teacher. "Do it anyway."

Children who are used to good literature frequently encounter
awful, voiceless writing on normative assessments.

Long Thinking

We make much of quick thinking: snappy repartee, the clever answer, the instant solution. Most tests are timed, and the right answer is predetermined. Quick thinking is an important aspect of any learner's profile.

However, most significant problems in research, social policy, government, or the arts are not solved quickly but require learners who can sustain their initiative from problem formulation to final solution.

We need thinkers who can come up with their own questions in their attempt to solve a problem. Once they have identified a relevant question, they need to know the right sources to consult for answers: read books, interview experts, gather data from the Internet. Finally, they need to be able to decide whether they've answered the question they've raised. Our learners need to know how to sustain thought on a single problem for days, weeks, or months—a skill that is developed over a lifetime.

At the moment our normative testing programs are interested only in quick thinking, and tests tend to govern how teachers teach. They are influenced by the format: multiple-choice questions, little, if any, writing required. So writing vanishes from the curriculum, replaced by lots of practice taking multiple-choice tests.

How are we encouraging long thinking in our classrooms?

Writing to a Prompt

Responding to a writing prompt isn't as simple or as valuable as it might seem. The usual advice to writers is to get right to the point, the center of the action. But this takes time and practice and the ability to select elements from a complete sequence.

Until children have had a lot of everyday writing experience and can relate the parts to the whole before they start, they will always be slow to get off the mark. Just as they must be able to arrange numbers in sequence before they can understand intervals, they must know which events follow other events in order to be able to focus on one moment in the sequence to the exclusion of the others.

For example, suppose a very young child wishes to write about the time he was lost on a mountain. He titles his story "Lost on a Mountain," but he begins by telling about getting out of bed, driving in the car, and arriving at the mountain. This long introduction may take from three to five pages. Indeed, the child is lost in this long entry. He then writes two paragraphs about being lost on the mountain, and one about the trip home. This is a typical bed-to-bed story. He must picture the entire trip, write his way into and away from the segment he wants to highlight. But it is often many years before children learn to do that.

The more sophisticated writer can begin with being lost on the top of the mountain: "A snowstorm swept in and quickly covered the cairns that marked the trail. We were on a hike through the Presidential mountains and we wondered how we'd find our way back." Then, for context and clarity, he can subordinate the necessary background material in subsequent paragraphs.

If children write daily and can put their finger on a place
in the text denoting the center of the action, they
will have come a long way to becoming writers.

Look How Well We're Doing!

I've always been uneasy about sending test data out of town so that someone who doesn't know my children can grade their reading skills. I get back a lot of numbers, but those numbers can't tell me what I need to do; the test is not diagnostic. There's nothing I can say other than, "You're doing fine." Or, "Try harder."

The real reason children are tested on the district, state, and national level is so the results can be used to assess the teacher. But which teacher? Maybe this year's teacher isn't so hot, but last year's was wonderful, and the current year's high scores are really the result of the prior teacher's work. And what about the makeup of the class? If 20 percent of the students were new and 15 percent weren't native speakers of English, any growth comparisons will be terribly skewed.

But school boards and administrators need to be able to tell the public how their children are improving. Realtors stand ready to post the scores on their web sites so that potential home buyers can see the supposed quality of local education. It's business and politics as usual, and our children are the ones who suffer.

We cannot wait for or expect people from out of town to assess our students—or trust them when they do. True assessment exists in the classroom; children need to know how to assess their own work.

A Child Shall Lead Us

Linda Rief did a study in the research course she took from me that turned my head and changed the way I viewed evaluation. She had a simple question, "What happens if we say the student is the most important evaluator?"

Linda got sixteen pieces of writing from a middle school in a nearby town. She asked her own students to rank the pieces from best to least best. Since they were new at being evaluators, she asked them to state why the top three and bottom three belonged where they were. Examining the ranked writing gave Linda a sense of where her students were as evaluators. She saw what she needed to do over the next eight weeks to help her students become better readers of other students' work as well as their own.

During the next eight weeks Linda's students ranked the work in their own folders and evaluated the work of other students in the class. They wrestled with the one thing various pieces were about. Whether something was good or had weaknesses, they had to suggest possibilities for improving the piece. Even (especially?) when a work was very poor, they had to hunt for a redeemable line, for something the author demonstrated he or she knew that could become the basis for improvement. Linda's focus was on the responsibility of the author to knowledgeably improve the work.

At the end of eight weeks the students evaluated sixteen more pieces of writing from a nearby school. This time the requirement was not only to rank the pieces but also to cite the strengths and weaknesses of each. As a control, Linda also had the sixteen pieces ranked by good writing teachers and by professional writers. The result? Linda's students did as well as good writing teachers, and a few were as effective as the professional writers.

Teachers need to stop being the only evaluator in the classroom; they need to spend far more time helping students read and critique their own work.

Seeing What It's Like

During my eighteen months of research on energy within the teaching profession, I kept in close touch with about a dozen educators. My usual approach was to preschedule a phone conversation in which I asked my questions and the person responded, or to e-mail a list of questions for the person to answer at his or her convenience.

On this particular morning I rang an elementary principal in Colorado. "What's new?"

"For starters our state board of education is requiring that each school must have a parent accountability council."

"Oh, no," I moaned sympathetically. "What will you have to put up with next?"

"Well, before you feel sorry for me, let me tell you what I did. I called for volunteers, with the stipulation that the parents had to take a sixth-grade reading test to see what it was like. I wouldn't score them; I'd just given them the answers as we went along and they could see for themselves how they were doing."

"What a brilliant idea!" I said.

"Well, we sat down together and they began reading those little paragraphs. Then I gave them the answers to the first five questions. You never heard such a commotion. 'That couldn't be the answer!' 'Three out of the five could have been right!' These parents were good readers and could see possibilities the authors of the test couldn't. They became so angry they challenged the state board of education to take the test.

"We worked very well together after that. And I think we came up with a sound approach to accountability."

Find a sample test and invite parents to take it.
Talk with them about what it felt like.

Independent Study

I sat in the Chief School Officer's study in Aberdeenshire, Scotland. I was there to exchange views about education. He wondered about my impressions of Scotland thus far. "In truth, sir, I've just come up from London and I'm just getting started."

"Ah, the English," he said. "They have their way, but we have ours here in Scotland, especially in Aberdeenshire. And I want you to know that when it comes to high honors, our students do very well when they go to England, or South Scotland." His eyes filled with merriment. (Later I would learn that the Scots jokingly called England "South Scotland.")

"Well then, how do you do it in Scotland?" I asked.

"Starting about age nine, the age of your third grade, we identify children's special interests and invite them to participate in what you call independent study. Throughout Aberdeenshire all teachers, including administrators, become tutors. My own special area is the American Civil War. The tutor and the child together come up with a study list. This study relationship continues through the rest of the child's schooling, through their A or O level exams. Believe it or not, some students study a third to a half of their subjects with a tutor. And those students do remarkably well on all their exams."

This perky Scot certainly turned my head about study and learning, and we had a good time in our subsequent discussion of the Civil War. What particularly struck me was that teachers, administrators, and students were all known for a special area of competence or interest.

What happens to a faculty, to a school, and to
the students when teachers, administrators, and
students are known for what they study and learn?

Competition

Lad Tobin, an accomplished English teacher who is now a professor at Boston College, hypothesizes that in any American classroom—elementary, secondary, or university—competition between students is part of the social climate. It's in the air.

In *Writing Relationships* (1993), Tobin writes, "At some point we designated competition a 'Devil term' and collaboration a 'God term,' without worrying about the fact that people sometimes collaborate to do terrible things or compete to do good. On what basis have we decided that collaboration and competition are mutually exclusive terms or that competition is necessarily bad for composition?"

Tobin points out that even in the best classrooms, because a teacher's approval is always part of the process, there is bound to be competition. Teachers can delay grades, always offer a positive response, but in the end what they say is important. Praise one child, and another yearns for that same praise—and perhaps comes to see that praise is a limited quantity. It is a long time indeed before any student, least of all a child, can say to himself about his teacher, "She's wrong and I am right about the quality of this piece."

Competition in the classroom is a fact. We need to reexamine the ways in which we promote it to the detriment of healthy learning.

Reporting to the Arabs

We already had report cards in Spanish, Macedonian, Serbo-Croatian, Polish, and Italian in the multiethnic neighborhood in which I was a supervisor. But that year a large number of our students were from Yemen and needed report cards in Arabic. I asked the director of a nearby settlement house if he knew anyone who could help us. "Yes, Mr. Hassan is from Yemen, and I believe he knows Arabic."

Mr. Hassan was a neat, quiet, well-dressed man who kept the books for the settlement house. I showed him the English version of the report card. On the left side the various skills were listed; there were columns to the right in which to check whether the child showed *strong, adequate,* or *minimal* improvement. Mr. Hassan smiled and said, "I'll have to be careful, because in Arabic the columns go from right to left, not left to right."

Two weeks later the report card was ready. The swoops, dots, and half moons characteristic of Arabic script were lovely to look at, but we had no way to verify the accuracy of what it said. We checked and double-checked that all the checkmarks on each child's card were in the correct columns.

Mary Alvira, the ESL teacher, asked me to remain at school with her on the day the children took the cards home. She was worried they might contain an inadvertent insult and unleash a protest. Twenty minutes after the cards went out, we heard a loud pounding on the school door. I stepped out to face a gathering crowd. Mohamed Mohamed waved a report card in the air. "Who has written this?"

I worried Mr. Hassan might be assaulted for his efforts. "I did," I responded. Well, I had at least checked the columns.

"You know Arabic?"

"Well, no. Mr. Hassan has written it."

Mohammed smiled and now said more quietly. "Oh, Mr. Graves, we must meet this man, for he is a poet."

Maybe we ought to have poets design and write all our report cards!

Learning Binges

Learning how to learn is being threatened by the pace of a school day stuffed with skill builders, worksheets, timed tests, and rapid transitions from one curriculum emphasis to another. In many "failing" schools recess has been abolished, along with art and music, in order to "cover" more material and boost standardized test scores. But hyperactivity is also endemic within upscale suburban communities. There are so many small pieces of curriculum attached to miniscule time intervals that significant learning, learning to think, is very much at risk.

Think of anything you know how to do well: weave, sing, crochet, make quilts, garden, interpret American history, hunt, fish, play an instrument, act in a play. The odds are you learned how to do this by going on a learning "binge." You spent hours outside the knowledge or skill until you found your way inside it. You thought about it even when you weren't actually doing it. Your mind continued to plan, work, and think, longing for the moment when you could again give the activity your full focus.

How well I remember Miss Adam's electrifying lesson on explorers in fifth grade. I raced home, changed my clothes and met my friend, Jimmy, to continue our game of explorers after school. I experienced one learning binge after another in succeeding years: bird study, hybridizing gladiolus, baseball, and memorizing silhouettes of World War II planes. Having parents and teachers who allowed me the luxury of pursuing my own learning contributed immeasurably to a lifetime of thinking and writing on which I subsequently embarked many years later.

Think of something you know how to do well.
How did you learn it? Who helped you?

The Power of A

Competition is the name of the game in most schools. Students find As in short supply. Administrators worry that their teachers are inflating grades. Here's another way to think about the matter.

"Grades say little about the work done. When you reflect to a student that he has misconstrued a concept or has taken a false step in a math problem, you are indicating something real about his performance, but when you give him a B+, you are saying nothing at all about his mastery of the material, you are only matching him up against other students. Most would recognize at core that the main purpose of grades is to compare one student with another." So say Rosamund Stone Zander and Benjamin Zander, in their book *The Art of Possibility* (2000).

"I tell [my students] that each student in the class will get an A for the course. 'However, there is one requirement that you must fulfill to earn this grade. Sometime during the next two weeks, you must write me a letter dated next May, which begins with the words, "Dear Mr. Zander, I got my A because . . ." and in this letter you are to tell in as much detail as you can about what happened to you that is in line with this extraordinary grade.' When the students write they place themselves in the future and report all the insights and learnings they've acquired during the year."

The Zanders' work could be adapted to younger learners to help them develop a vision of becoming and of seeing within themselves the emerging learner. I remember as a child saying to my mother when she read to me each day, "Mom, when will I be able to read this all by myself?" The feeling of what it was like to hold a book and read it was already germinating.

Choose two or three children and ask them to describe themselves
as learners who have already achieved their dreams.

Problem Finding

Back in 1979 I read a book that led me to a new paradigm for thinking about children and learning. In *The Creative Vision: A Longitudinal Study of Problem Finding in Art* (1976), Jacob Getzels and Mihaly Csikszentmihalyi detailed research revealing qualities that could be used to predict which artists who graduated from the University of Chicago art school would be successful.

Basically, they distinguished two kinds of thinkers, problem solvers and problem finders. The problem finders became successful, independent artists. The authors write: "In principle the same problem-finding paradigm seems to apply to forms of creativity other than the artistic. Time and again outstanding scientists have stated that the formulation of a problem is more essential than its solution, and that it is a more imaginative act."

Applying this to public education I ask: How often do we put children in the position of being problem finders rather than problem solvers? How often do we tell children, "I suspect you have a partial solution for this problem you've raised. Think about it and work on it again. It will come to you." Or, "Tell your problem to a friend, give your partial solution, talk it over. Maybe two heads are better than one."

Unfortunately, current approaches to testing are rarely concerned with problem finding; the questions asked are those to which the test maker already knows the answers. Problem solving is important, but isn't problem finding at least its equal and therefore in need of far more application?

How can you help your students become problem finders?

PART NINE

Full Circle

The final days of the year are a time to concentrate on our classroom again, to review the year, to continue to interact with the children. The sense of energy and excitement we feel reminds us of September. It is also time for a little humor. Sometimes the things that irritate us most we need to spoof.

Now is also the time to help our children appreciate what they have learned and enjoyed this year. We review favorite books, examine our best writing together, celebrate science projects, apply math to real-life problems. Maybe we present an art exhibit. Or make up lists of our favorites—songs, stories, pastimes, whatever. We've had a good year together. Let's enjoy the memories!

Looking Back at Community

Building a classroom community is sophisticated work and can require extraordinary effort. If we've been teaching in the same school for a number of years, the work goes more easily. If we are new in a building, we have to start from scratch.

I learn all my students' names before they even enter the room. Within two days I want to be able to put faces with those names. I also immediately try to notice something special about each person. I make it a point to accompany the children wherever they go—to lunch, special classes, the playground. I need to see them in as many different situations as possible.

When students are working at their seats I roam the room attending to skills, seeing what individual children know, what emotions they reveal in their work and in their interactions. I speak loudly enough so that the children nearby will hear: "I see you know how to use quotation marks. Tell me how you know how to do that." "You are reading about sharks. How did you get interested in sharks?" "What are you planning to learn next?"

Some teachers develop the ability to notice emotions, skills, and interests instantly. If one has over a hundred students, an observational shorthand perhaps becomes instinctive. But it is a highly refined skill that too few teachers possess.

Teachers set the tone for building community; they learn as much about the children as possible and attend to how they feel and what they know already.

R-E-S-P-E-C-T

I have only a few goals for classroom behavior, and respecting one another is at the head of the list. This means I have to be the first to demonstrate, in word and deed, what I mean by respect.

A child brings in a cricket for the science center. "Thank you for your contribution, Mark." Gratitude is at the root of courtesy and is also a great energizer. I may not feel like saying thank you (we already have a lot of crickets), but I know that the words lead me in the right direction—respect for Mark's action of bringing something in.

Another child, Stephen, says, "Hah, we've already got a thousand crickets."

"Okay, Stephen, how can you make your point and still show Mark respect? You obviously feel differently about this."

"I do. I feel like he doesn't, well, he doesn't know our situation."

"So you're perplexed? Confused? Maybe you could thank him for the cricket, then express how you feel. Try it now."

"Okay. Thank you for the cricket, Mark, but I feel like we have so many. So how come you brought this one in?"

"Well, I heard that our frogs had big appetites and maybe we needed more."

I reinforce the language of respect. "Thank you both for helping me understand both your points of view."

Teaching respect takes long, slow, patient work but in the
long run provides a real source of energy for the class.

161 Delegate!

Children should take responsibility for the general running of their classroom. There are always issues of tidiness, organization, visitor protocol, and field-trip arrangements and finances. These jobs should rotate, and the children need to be shown how to handle the responsibility. In many cases the last child to hold the job can introduce the new person to its requirements.

The more children or students have responsibility for making a room hum productively, the more they appreciate how groups work together. When I visit a classroom, I'm delighted when one of the students explains what they are doing: "And this is how our room works. Only three people to a group, and these books are for science, and over here we have a craft area. And look over at the teacher. She is meeting with one of the children about the paper he's written."

Grade-level meetings in which teachers share what they've successfully delegated to the students are tremendously helpful. "You mean you've been able to get your students to handle that?" I know one teacher who was able to have a student schedule writing conferences for her in second grade!

Delegating responsibilities builds class cohesiveness
and gives students a sense of place.

That Group Feeling

I've noticed that classrooms in which children do things together like singing, choral speaking, marching, putting on a play, or organizing a science fair feel more cohesive. The children have an energy that makes them sparkle. They say with pride, "In *our* class we do thus-and-so."

I used to achieve that group feeling through choral speaking. I first picked it up from Dr. Doris Edins, in Buffalo. I watched her teach choral speaking to first graders. I couldn't believe how quickly they learned three poems without any texts to refer to. "That's the secret," Edins said. "Poetry is meant to come in through the ear. I say the poem through once, then I repeat the first two lines. Next I say, 'Watch my mouth and feel it with me.' Then we say it together. I tell them, 'And after those first two lines we say together, you just say any words you remember.' The amazing thing is that there are always three or four children who know some part of it, so that the children feel they have become an instant chorus. Two or three more repetitions and they'll have the full poem." I tried the Edins approach (of course, *I* had to memorize the poems first), and it worked.

In the course of a day there are all kinds of moments when choral speaking can become a real source of energy and camaraderie—waiting for the art teacher to come, getting ready to go out to the busses, heading off to the lunchroom.

Choral speaking, singing, or any ritual that a class enjoys together can be a source of energy and promote a feeling of togetherness.

In Someone Else's Shoes

Understanding other points of view is one of the benchmarks of becoming a mature person. We spend a lifetime trying to understand other points of view.

I was in a second grade gathering data when the children tumbled back into class from recess. Their cheeks were red and their eyes were blazing as they doffed their jackets and snow boots. "What seems to be the trouble?" I asked.

"The fifth graders are picking on the little kids."

"They kicked our balls over the fence."

"They pushed us into the snow."

"What a minute," I said. "Let's get some of this down here on paper. Come over here by the easel."

The children had no trouble coming up with additional offenses. The list grew quickly. When it had been completed, I drew a line under it and said, "Now pretend you are the fifth graders, and let's come up with their list of what happened."

From their startled looks, I knew they thought I'd gone over to the fifth graders' side. "No, I believe you," I said, "but there must have been some reason that the fifth graders did these things." They remained mute. "Do you suppose I should bring some of them down so you could ask them?"

"No, that wouldn't be a good idea," one said.

"'Cuz they'll beat us up afterward."

So they tried to see their list from the perspective of the fifth graders.

"Maybe they didn't have balls of their own to play with."

"Maybe they just did it because we're smaller than they are. Or maybe fifth graders did it to them when they were in second grade."

Empathy with another person's point of view is one of the building blocks of good writing as well as a democratic society. Think of ways to help your students see beyond their own side of things.

"You're on Your Own"

Eighty teachers, three television cameras, and a forest of cables and klieg lights surrounded Mary Ellen Giacobbe and a dozen second graders during a demonstration writing lesson. The children were busy drawing and writing. A boy came up to Mary Ellen.

"My stapler is jammed, Mrs. Giacobbe."

Mary Ellen never misses an opportunity to help children be independent. "That's interesting, Andrew. What can you do about that? I'm sure you'll figure some way to solve the problem." And off she went to confer with other children about their writing.

Curious about what he would do, I watched Andrew go back to his work area. He looked at the stapler, realized he couldn't solve the jam, and got six paper clips to hold two large pieces of paper together.

We too often solve problems for children instead
of letting them solve them on their own.

The School of Hard Knocks

Whenever I want to get a conversation going in a workshop, I say, "Tell me about how your day gets interrupted." Teachers race to trump one another: "You think that's bad, listen to this." A number of their complaints have found their way into the following play in one act.

A classroom during writing time. The teacher walks up to a student and looks down at his paper.

<u>Teacher:</u> I see you're writing about whales. Can you tell me a little more here about—*(Knock on door)* Come in. *(Child holding slip of paper steps into room)* What have you got there? *(Child hands paper to teacher)* "There will be a faculty meeting at three-fifteen. Attendance is required. Check next to your name." *(Teacher turns back to class)* Who was I talking with?

<u>Child Writing About Whales:</u> With me.

<u>Teacher:</u> I can't remember what we were talking about. What were you writing? *(Another knock on door)* What?

<u>Voice in the Hall:</u> Where's Agatha? She's late.

<u>Teacher:</u> Oh, I'm sorry. Samantha, you were supposed to remind Agatha to go to the reading room at nine-ten so I wouldn't be interrupted! On your way, Agatha. *(To child sitting two seats behind writer-about-whales)* What were we just talking about?

<u>Child:</u> I don't know. You weren't speaking with me.

<u>Voice on Loudspeaker:</u> Now hear this. It is March and raining and the playground is muddy. The children should wipe their feet carefully before coming in or Mr. Rose is going to quit.

<u>Teacher</u> *(to no one in particular)*: What day is today? What time is it? *(Another knock on door)* What now?! Who is it and what's your business?

<u>Voice in the Hall:</u> Sara is supposed to be in the guidance office.

<u>Teacher</u> *(near tears)*: Sara, why didn't you go to guidance? Why?? You know what? You stay. I'm going to guidance. Good-bye to you all!!

Anything sound familiar?

Learning to Ask Questions

In the school where I was principal, each child researched a topic of special interest. We called it *specialty reporting,* after the work of Dr. Donald D. Durrell, of Boston University. The children read about their topic, interviewed someone who knew more about the subject than they did, and made a presentation or constructed a model.

The children did their research and wrote up the questions they would ask in their interviews. When I listened in, I noticed that even if the respondent answered all their other questions in answering the first one, they still continued doggedly through their list. Clearly, they weren't really listening to their expert; asking the questions was all that mattered. I decided the children needed more practice.

I set up a little area outside my office framed by a picket fence. Then I called in a series of volunteers from the community, whom children, in teams of two or three, would come and interview. We had people who knew about lobsters, deep-sea fishing, whales, scallop dragging, milking cows, knitting, furniture refinishing, people who had traveled to interesting places. Each "expert" and subject area was advertised well in advance, and there was a sign-up sheet. I told the experts they were only to answer the questions the children asked and offer no other information. That way, the children would have to listen more carefully and learn how to follow one question with an appropriate next one.

Waves of children participated in the interviews, and it wasn't long before some started competing to see who could come up with the best "scoop," the most unique piece of information or fact.

How often does your class or school draw on the resources
of the community? How could you begin?

Students See, Students Do

When I taught seventh grade I treated report writing as a rite of passage. The papers had to be twelve pages long, cite at least three references, and have a bibliography. I gave students eight weeks to complete the report. On Monday of each week I intoned in an ominous voice, "You have thus-and-so weeks left." Of course, to a twelve- or thirteen-year-old, eight weeks in the future is never-never land.

(Want firsthand proof? One Saturday morning day my son Bill, then the same age as these seventh graders, slipped in a matter-of-fact request. "Dad, do you suppose we could swing by the library on your way shopping?"

I was impressed. "What's the deal at the library?"

"Got a report due."

"When did you get the assignment?"

"Oh, I forget."

"Is it due Monday?"

"Yeah." Then, catching my look, he blurted, "Geez, Dad, today is Saturday. I've got two whole days!")

Anyway. Back to teaching report writing. Probably only three out of the thirty students could have done the assignment on their own. So I demonstrated the process by writing a report of my own during those eight weeks. I selected a topic, went to the library, took notes, listed my key questions, wrote and edited my draft. And I kept them moving along on their reports as I progressed with mine.

Camille Allen, in her book *The Multigenre Research Paper* (2001), shows the power of teachers and children working together over time to achieve a new kind of excellence in report writing. Check it out.

How will you will show your students your thought
processes for writing a report or a project?

The Secretary of Education Pays a Visit

In the 1980s the school in which I was conducting research was going to be presented with the Flag of Excellence by the Secretary of Education, Mr. William Bennett. It was also the year of the two hundredth anniversary of the U. S. Constitution. Word came that Mr. Bennett wanted to demonstrate a lesson on the U. S. Constitution in a third-grade class.

We scratched our collective heads. Why the third grade? The children probably wouldn't have even heard of the Constitution much less know what's in it. The third-grade teachers drew straws; the lot fell to Paula Walsh, an outstanding teacher. Paula had a week to introduce the Constitution and the concept of a codified document governing behavior. She did so in the context of the rules that applied to the classroom and the playground, stressing that the Constitution was a larger version containing "guidelines for the entire country."

Secretary Bennett entered the school preceded by two secret service agents and followed by another. Advance investigators had double-checked the security of the school. Three national television channels were covering the event. There was no space in the classroom for observers, so we watched on a closed-circuit monitor in another room.

"What's in the U. S. Constitution?" asked Bennett. Ten hands went up. "Yes." He pointed to a child.

"Don't punch anyone out." Flabbergasted, Bennett nevertheless continued. "Yes."

"Don't walk on the grass." Sweat poured down Bennett's face, and it wasn't just from the lights. "One more."

"People should help each other."

"That's good," Bennett said with some relief. Not about to chance any more statements from the children with three network cameras rolling, he spent the next twenty minutes telling the children what was in the Constitution.

Think of a time your students were totally
baffled by something you tried to teach.

What's It For?

One of my graduate students was conducting research. When the children she was observing were in the midst of writing, she'd ask, "What's this for?" and point to the paper on the desk.

Most children replied something like this: "Oh, this is for the teacher. I'll give it to her when I'm done." But a few answered along these lines: "I'm working on this because I want to find out how it is going to end." The latter answer shows a sense of function and personal ownership: *this is for me*.

I asked the graduate student to ask the classroom teacher the same question "just out of curiosity." Later she reported the teacher had said, "Oh, the paper is for the children." Isn't it interesting that each thought the writing was for the other? It could be that these particular children were not developmentally advanced enough to understand the function of writing, or it could be that the writing being done in that classroom was too teacher-directed.

Anthropologists ask questions about function and ownership in any culture they are trying to understand: "What can you do with this thing, and who are the people authorized to use it?"

We need to help children understand that
writing and reading belong to them.

Lively Learning

For a workshop on curriculum I conducted with the teachers in an elementary school, I wanted to make the point that most schools are surrounded by lively resources that can be drawn on in all aspects of school curriculum. I decided to highlight resources that were no more than a three-minute walk from the school.

I did some legwork in advance. I went across the street to the Methodist church and found a woman who was an expert on stained-glass windows. She sent me across the street to an antiques dealer, who lived in his shop, which was next door to the school. I learned that everything in his home except for the TV set was an antique. He had period bedrooms, some of the furniture dating back to 1750. The school was adjacent to a veritable museum, yet no teacher or administrator had ever asked whether groups of children could tour his home. His only dealings with the school were to toss back the balls that sometimes sailed over the fence into his garden. Within my three-minute circumference I also discovered a German-speaking gardener, a jazz saxophonist, a ham radio operator, and a woman who owned thousand-year-old Chinese tapestries. There were also people who had emigrated from or traveled to all parts of the world.

When the teachers gathered for the workshop, I told them to keep their coats on (it was January, in western New York). I assigned them to teams of three people each and passed out envelopes to each team. In the envelopes were instructions like this one:

> Mr. Karl Kranz, at Kranz antiques, next door to the school, is expecting you to visit at 9:15 in order to learn all you can about bureaus in the American colonies between 1750 and 1800. You have thirty minutes. From 9:45 until 10:15 your team will have a chance to figure out how you will teach what you have just learned to others. Then from 10:15 until 10:45 you will teach three different groups what you have learned.

There is nothing like the living curriculum of information
shared by someone who knows a subject firsthand.

Loving History

Roger Mudd was interviewing the eminent historian David McCullough on the History Channel one evening.

"As a history teacher, what did you hope for your students?" asked Mudd.

"I hoped that every student would fall in love with history."

"How did you do that?"

"If my students are to fall in love with history, they have to discover it. Say I'm teaching about turn-of-the-century American history. I pass out artifacts about that period, like something from Ellis Island, a Scott Joplin score, a painting, a letter or document. My students are to take that artifact and use it as a lens to understand the history of the period. When they come to class they share their findings. Each of them feels as though they are learning something unique. The more they follow their trail, the better the discovery gets."

There is no energizer like getting lost in a subject.

Before You Add, Subtract

Many people seem to think the school day is like an accordion file: it will expand to accommodate whatever is added. Unfortunately, the school day and year is the same length today as it was seventy years ago, and in that time curriculum has expanded tenfold.

Each year someone stands up and says, "This year the new addition to our curriculum will be thus-and-so. We also have to make sure we get higher scores."

When I speak to large groups of teachers I often ask, "Is anyone here going to retire this year?" Two or three hands will usually be raised.

Then I say, "Would one of you be willing to make a sacrifice for the sake of the rest of the faculty? At the next curriculum meeting, when someone wants to add something new, ask, "What are we going to drop in order to make room for it? There is no time left in the day!" I get my laugh.

I go on to make my point. "Those of you who are not going to retire need to ask this same question. The school day is filled to the brim and beyond. Choices need to be made. Just be sure you act as a team. If you're the only one to ask, it may seem as if you're the only disgruntled teacher."

Additions to the curriculum require an evaluation
of how time is used and of what can be dropped.

Let Children Show the Way

I have a simple way to get the lay of the land in the classrooms I visit. I ask one child to take me around the room and explain how things work. Again and again I ask the anthropologist's question: *What's that for?*

We pass a collection of books. "What are these for?"

"Those are science books, and sometimes when we study a unit we pass those around, but there aren't enough copies for everyone to read at one time."

"And these books over here?"

"These books are organized by how hard they are to read. The reds are much harder than the greens or yellows."

"And what is your teacher doing over there?"

"She's meeting with three children who are reading the same book. She asks them questions and then she talks to them about what they'll do next."

"Why are they doing that?"

"Well, some kids like to read the same book, and they can discuss it before they get to meet with the teacher."

"How do you keep track of all the things going on in this room? Isn't it confusing?"

"We have our own records where we write down what we read and write, and you'd better keep it up-to-date. If we need help we know who to go to. But you can't have more than three talking together at one time."

"I see. So there are limits?"

Ask a trusted colleague to ask your students what things are for and what the limits are. Then do the same for your colleague.

Learning Interrupted

Classroom interruptions work against the group feeling we try to build in our learning communities.

I once tried to record the number of interruptions that took place in a classroom I was observing. After eight interruptions in fifteen minutes, I gave up. You know the list: two intercom messages from the front office, two children leaving for music lessons, one going to the nurse about a suspicious rash, two notes from other teachers, one child off to reading clinic. Teachers and children are so used to interruptions that they become a way of life outside the classroom as well as in it.

Is there anything we can do about it?

Well, one teacher put a sign up in the window portion of her door: *PLEASE DO NOT INTERRUPT OUR LEARNING.*

A high school teacher, a crusty, experienced teacher with white hair, had one of her students write down every classroom interruption that took place during a week's time. Then she showed the list to her principal and asked, "If you say that learning is the most important thing that's going on here in my room, then what is your interpretation of this list?"

Instructional time should rarely be interrupted. Write down how many times you are interrupted, by what or whom.

Recess

I am fascinated by the social playground that is recess, by the expressions of self that explode after being caged within the confines of the classroom. Games spring into instantaneous being: "I'm up first." "I pitch first. You be on my team." Or teams continue yesterday's game, the score dutifully remembered. Naturally, arguments ensue: "Safe!" "Out!" "Safe I say!" "Wanna make something of it?" A group of children gathers to talk intimately about personal matters. Others stand warily on the fringes waiting for an invitation that sometimes never comes. A few children stick close to the teacher, never leaving her side.

To the people who wish to abolish recess for the sake of academic success, I say, "Get out on the playground and join a team." When I do intense thinking I need a break. After I've written for an hour, I'll weed in the garden or play solitaire—my versions of doing something completely different. The intensity of learning has to be broken by recreation. I wrote this poem about the joy and drama of kickball:

Kickball

Michael ran and planted
One foot like it wouldn't budge
In a hurricane, stuck out
His tongue, and swung
That other leg ripping
Rubber right off the ball,
And BOOM a sound was heard
Clear into Ms. Winter's
Room; the ball sailed high,

A high like something shot
From a cannon down at the circus.
Michael pumped around those bases,
Laughing and waving his arms
Hoping recess would go on for hours
And hours, and he didn't care
If he ever got to home plate
Just so home runs would never end.

*Choose one child who interests you and watch
an entire recess through that child's eyes.*

Troubleshooting

There are times when a lesson isn't working; there's too much noise, or organizational structures we've instituted for the classroom have broken down.

When this happens, I call a class meeting, because this is both the children's room and mine. Or sometimes the students ask for a class meeting. The purpose of the meeting is to get the facts behind the problem. No names are used, no blame assigned. This isn't a witch-hunt.

"Today I want to talk about the book area. There seems to be some confusion about getting the books back in the right place. What are the facts?"

"There's not enough shelf space, and we have to stuff the books in."

"We have a lot of new books."

"What are your ideas for solving this problem?"

"We need a larger bookcase."

"We don't have any money for one."

"My dad has one made out of just bricks and boards. That's cheap."

"Guess we have a solution."

Children must be able to solve the real problems that occur in their classroom; this is fundamental to understanding life in a democracy.

This Land Is Our Land

In one of the schools in which I taught, the primary classes studied a plot of land that had been marked off with surveyor's tape. It was about twenty feet by twenty feet of rough "unused" ground and included one tree. There were small areas of sand to capture the tracks of creatures large or small (in the winter, snow also served this function). Two pathways cut the plot into rough quarters and also allowed access to the interior portions.

The children investigated what was happening to and on this plot of land several times a week throughout the school year. Small groups were assigned to record—with sketches, photographs, and careful notes—everything they noticed in their quadrant. They catalogued the various plants and insects; identified squirrel, vole, and mouse tracks; noted evidence of disease and the effects of drought or heavy rain; etc. When the leaves began to change in the fall, teachers took digital photos of the same leaf each day in order to document the change as the green chlorophyll was used up and the colors beneath were revealed. They also took digital photos in the spring when the leaves grew back.

The discovery quotient was high. Interest waned a bit during the hard, cold months of January and February but perked up again as soon as the weather got warmer.

There is nothing like studying a plot of land over the course of a year to develop good observation habits and a sense of nature.

Our Faces, Our Teaching

I often ponder the messages we send our students as we teach. Do our words match our facial expressions? What are we saying with our hands, our posture, the position of our arms, how close or far away we stand? When we're having a bad day, does it show?

When savvy teachers enter a new classroom, they immediately crouch down so that they are at the children's eye level. They approach individual children to chat or look at the work on the child's desk. They are careful to respect children's sense of personal space.

Towering over children and issuing commands sends another message altogether.

Do we present a pleasant face in the classroom?
What expressions might a video camera capture?

Think About Publishing

"I could write a book about that," you say in half jest to a colleague, "but I just don't have the time." Publishers are looking for people who can write and more teachers are publishing than ever before. Few can start with a book but many teachers can begin with a page, a two-page commentary, or a short article.

Every day, classrooms are filled with stories that other teachers need to read about and understand. You have tried something new and it works. The real story is not in the tip but in what you learned. Every day we try things that don't work. Show why it didn't and tell what you learned.

You don't have the time? Choose a safe, ten-minute spot in the day. Brainstorm and let all things in about your choice of topic. At the end of the week try several times to write what the one thing your brainstorming is about. Next, lower your standards and write about the "one thing" for ten minutes nonstop. Write a letter to a colleague about your one thing. Put in the details that were missing when you wrote quickly. Be sure to mail this letter or send it on e-mail.

Later, ask her what she thinks the piece is about and why. Above all, ask her where she thinks she heard your heartbeat, your main feelings in the piece. Finally, ask her what she wants to know more about.

Stories and ideas for writing occur every day in your classroom. Commit yourself to a discipline of writing each day. In time, after good response from friends and able colleagues, your work will be published.

Our Favorite Things

Here's a fun end-of-year game your class can play as a way to review the year.

First, have them list the books they have read or heard you read aloud. (They may already have such a list in their folders, if they keep a running tally during the year.) Let them go to the bookshelves or the school library to refresh their memories. Older children may wish to include authors as well as titles and categorize their list by genre: fiction, nonfiction, historical fiction, information books, poetry, etc.

Next, have the children put stars by their top five favorite books. They can also indicate their top five favorite authors, top five favorite characters (from fiction and biographies), five most interesting nonfiction subjects, whatever categories you identify.

Then create committees to review the "ballots" and create a master list for each category. Finally ask the children to choose their top three from each master list.

After the final results have been posted, discuss together what about the most popular choices may have made them so popular.

Children will love a chance to show how much they value
the books they have heard, read, or shared with friends.

REFERENCES

Allen, Camille. 2001. *The Multigenre Research Paper: Voice, Passion, and Discovery in Grades 4–6.* Portsmouth, NH: Heinemann.

Bennis, Warren, and Robert J. Thomas. 2002. *Geeks and Geezers: How Era, Values, and Defining Moments Shape Leaders.* Boston: Harvard Business School Press.

Bruner, Jerome. 1962. *The Process of Education.* Cambridge: Harvard University Press.

Covey, Stephen R. 1989. *Seven Habits of Highly Effective People.* New York: Simon and Schuster.

Elbow, Peter. 1998. "The Believing Game." *Writing Without Teachers.* Oxford University Press.

Getzels, Jacob W., and Mihaly Csikszentmihalyi. 1976. *The Creative Vision: A Longitudinal Study of Problem Finding in Art.* New York: John Wiley and Sons.

Graves, Donald H. 1987. *Experiment with Fiction.* Portsmouth, NH: Heinemann.

———. 1987. *Investigate Nonfiction.* Portsmouth, NH: Heinemann.

———. 1992. *Explore Poetry.* Portsmouth, NH: Heinemann.

———. 1995. *Baseball, Snakes and Summer Squash: Poems About Growing Up.* Hinsdale, PA: Wordsong/Boyds Mills.

———. 1998. *How to Catch a Shark.* Portsmouth, NH: Heinemann.

———. 1999. *Bring Life into Learning.* Portsmouth, NH: Heinemann.

———. 2001. *The Energy to Teach.* Portsmouth, NH: Heinemann.

———. 2002. *Testing Is Not Teaching: What Should Count in Education.* Portsmouth, NH: Heinemann.

Gruber, Ruth. 2003. *Inside of Time: My Journey from Alaska to Israel.*

Kittle, Penny. 2003. *Public Teaching One Kid at a Time.* Portsmouth, NH: Heinemann.

Marsalis, Wynton. Dec. 1995. "In Their Own Words." Speech to the National Press Club, Washington, DC.

Pedersen, Eigil, Therese Annette Faucher, and William Eaton. 1978. "A New Perspective on the Effects of First-Grade Teachers on Children's Subsequent Adult Status." *Harvard Educational Review* 48 (1).

Rogovin, Paula. 1998. *Classroom Interviews.* Portsmouth, NH: Heinemann.

———. 2001. *The Research Workshop.* Portsmouth, NH: Heinemann.

Simon, Neil. 1992. "The Art of the Theatre." *Paris Review* 125 (Winter).

Smith, Frank. 1982. *Writing and the Writer.* New York: Holt, Rinehart & Winston.

Stone, Irving. 1980. *The Origin.* New York: Doubleday.

Thomas, Lewis. 1979. *The Medusa and the Snail: More Notes of a Biology Watcher.* New York: Viking.

Wheatley, Margaret. 1999. *Leadership and the New Science.* San Francisco: Berrett-Koehler.

Wiener, Leo. 1967. *Tolstoy on Education.* Chicago: University of Chicago Press.

Zander, Rosamund Stone, and Benjamin Zander. 2000. *The Art of Possibility.* Boston: Harvard Business School Press.

Zymborska, Wislawa. 1996. "The Poet and the World." Nobel Laureate address. Stockholm.

Donald H. Graves has been involved in writing research for two decades. His books *Writing: Teachers & Children at Work* (Heinemann, 1983) and *A Fresh Look at Writing* (Heinemann, 1994) are best-sellers throughout the English-speaking world and have revolutionized the way writing is taught in schools. His most recent publications from Heinemann include the 20th Anniversary Edition of *Writing* (2003), *Testing Is Not Teaching* (2002), *The Energy to Teach* (2001), and *Bring Life into Learning: Create a Lasting Literacy* (1999). A former teacher, school principal, and language supervisor, Dr. Graves is Professor Emeritus at the University of New Hampshire. He also conducts workshops and speaks to teachers as part of Heinemann's Professional Development program.